I0569938

EZEKIEL SAW
THE WHEEL

CAN YOU SEE THE CROSS?

Universal Revelations

WILLIE JAMES WEBB

EZEKIEL SAW THE WHEEL: Can You See The Cross?
Universal Revelations
Copyright © 2024 by Willie James Webb

ISBN: 9798-9907506-4-7 PB
ISBN: 9798-9907506-5-4 HB

All rights reserved. No part of this publication may be reproduced,
distributed, or transmitted in any form or by any means, including
photocopying, recording, or other electronic or mechanical methods,
without the prior written embodied in critical elites and cera, open in
hovered rise permitted by copyright law.

Although every precaution has been taken to verify the accuracy of the
information contained herein, the author/publisher assumes no
responsibility for any errors or omissions. No liability is assumed for
damages that may result from the use of information contained within.

Printed in the United States of America
Independently Published by Willie James Webb

DEDICATION

This book is dedicated to Educator Booker T. Washington, Evangelist Billy Graham and Civil Rights Leader Martin Luther King, Jr., three men who never held public office, whose lives exemplify the highest expressions of Christian ethics and American values for the common good of America and for all humanity. May the glory of God continue to shine through their legacy.

Willie James Webb

CONTENTS

PREFACE

The most significant document known to mankind was written over two thousand years ago. Not only is it the most significant document, but it is the most vital and relevant document for the survival of mankind. It is the greatest sourcebook about human beings and human nature known to man. It is a sourcebook with more authority than any other book. It is the most credible book known to mankind.

It is the primary sourcebook about the creation of the universe and human life. It is the primary sourcebook about the purpose of human life and human purpose. It is the most authoritative book about God, the Creator. It is the only credible book containing explicitly the will of God for individual, Group, Corporate, National and global human lives and human living.

It is most amazing about the most amazing book, that it was written over two thousand years ago, covering a writing period of over 1600 (sixteen hundred) years with over 40 writers. This amazement is highlighted when we consider the relatively primitive environment in which the Bible was developed and written. This was a pre-scientific, pre-modern and pre-enlightenment age. There was no semblance of electricity, electronics, motor vehicles, no telephone, no telegraph, no electric light, no printing press, no thoughts of aviation. These were the days of riding on the backs of animals, or carts, wagons or sleds pulled by animals.

God revealed himself and his purpose for mankind more thoroughly, completely and with more finality in this relatively primitive, rudimentary environment than he has with all of our modern, scientific and space-age knowledge. It is also amazing that not only has this scientific knowledge age not invalidated the truth of the Bible. Scientific knowledge and this scientific age are validating the truth of the Bible. True science, valid art, valid law and valid religion lead us to the true word of God found in the Bible.

The truth of the matter is, that modern man is lagging dangerously behind the Bible, ethically, morally, spiritually, socially, economically and politically. If we do not catch up in these six areas of living, alluded to, modern technology or the misuse of modern technology will end up destroying civilization. Although the Bible may have come out of the dark ages, it is the brightest light that civilization has for the new modern age.

It is sad to say and an indictment to acknowledge, the respect and reverence for the Bible and the study of the Bible is grossly neglected by the church, educational institutions, health and government agencies. This failure to take the Bible seriously is being done out of callous ignorance, presumptuous thinking and spiritual arrogance. This is an attitude that does not know; assuming there is no need to know and pretending that it is not important to know. The prophet Hosea responded to this spiritual ignorance and arrogance when he stated these scathing words: "My people are destroyed for lack of knowledge; because thou hast rejected knowledge, I will also reject thee, that thou shall be no priest to me: seeing thou hast forgotten the law of thy God, I will also forget thy children." (Hosea 4:6). The words of the prophet Hosea are very harsh. However, there are detrimental consequences that are passed on to children as well as the oncoming generation when we neglect the word and law of God.

Centuries later when Jesus was rejected by Jerusalem, he expressed a similar sentiment, "If thou hadst known, even thou, at least in this thy day, the things which belong unto thy peace! For the days shall come upon thee, that thine enemies shall cast a trench about thee, and compass thee round, and keep thee in on every side. And shall lay thee even with the ground, and thy children within thee..." (Luke 19:42-44). Jesus is giving warning of the dire consequences of rejecting the message and the word that became flesh from God. This willful ignorance, arrogance and antichrist (1 John 4:1-3) spirit is an ongoing, deepening tragedy, even in the scientific day, two thousand years after the coming of Jesus Christ.

Ezekiel Saw the Wheel-Can You See the Cross, is a book that confronts graphically, artfully, scientifically, lawfully, ethnically and spiritually the ignorance, callousness and arrogance toward the revelatory message of God contained in the Bible. The anti-God, anti-Christ and anti-Bible attitudes are rampant in American society, as well as in other parts of the world. Some Laws prohibit The Ten Commandments in government buildings. Some laws prohibit the Nativity Scene on public property. Judges have ruled that crosses are religious symbols and must not be on the gravesite of National cemeteries for war veterans.

There are anti-Christ spirits that advocate taking the name of Christ out of Christmas songs. There are anti-Christ spirits who seek to prohibit hotels from having Bibles in their hotel rooms.

Part of the motivation behind writing this book is to present as graphically as I can the solid invincible facts, truth and solid evidence of God's revelation of himself in his creation, in the Bible and in Jesus Christ. God has given me innumerable revelations of the cross. Two trees over seventy feet high fell in the back area of my house within a four-week period of time. These large trees fell in a cross formation. It was not only fascinating to me, but I saw a message in this cross formed by the two fallen trees.

There are many examples and manifestations of the cross. In the State Capitol Building of Georgia, I noticed that there were very distinct crosses on the interior office doors. I asked several in the Capitol Building whether they saw anything unusual or distinct about the doors inside the Capitol. They did not see those distinct and vivid crosses on those doors that I saw. I am not aware as to whether the crosses on those doors are by intentional design or just coincidental. Nevertheless, they are there. I am convinced that there are visible revelations and messages around us that we do not see. By the same token, there are angelic sounds and speech that we don't hear. This is a time when it is vitally important to attune our spiritual radar to receive God's messages and revelations.

In spite of the horrific tragedy that took place on September 11, 2011, in the heart of New York City, a large metal cross was found in the rubble of the demolished trade center that revived hope. The discovery of this large metal cross inspired the production of a 54-minute film entitled, The Cross and the Towers. (2006 Atlas Asset Management Co.). The discovery of this cross inspired hope and changed lives for the better. The cross does have a religious significance; however, the cross is not restricted to religion or Christianity. Even, if it were restricted as a religious symbol, what rational justification would there be to ban the cross from Public facilities?

However. this book will leave no doubt in the minds of rational people, that the cross is a universal symbol. It goes back beyond the time of Christianity. This book will leave no room for doubt, that the cross is so prevalent and interwoven in the human environment and in God's creation, that it cannot be banned. Because there are too many intersections, crossroads, crossties, compasses, plus signs and time signs, airplanes and birds that replicate the cross. The cross cannot be successfully banned. It is a part of the erect human skeletal frame and structure. It is built into creation, north, south. east and west.

There is an inherent relationship between man and the earth. The 24-hour day and night accommodates the working (awakening) and sleeping patterns of man and other animals as well. The body of man requires a certain number of hours of sleep and rest within the 24-hour day in order to maintain health. The earth is a food, water, and oxygen source to sustain life. The earth has a delicately balanced ecological environment conducive to the existence and sustenance of plant and animal life. It is obvious that the relationship between man and the earth which creates an environment conducive for life was not accidental or haphazard. There is an intelligent design for the purpose of nurturing and sustaining life on the earth. There is a divine, creative and powerful intelligence that is "mindful" of man and "cares" about man. The religious, artful, lawful and scientific evidence confirms this loving divine Intelligence for mankind. This complementary and accommodative relationship is explained fully and completely in the Bible. God's creation and God's revelation are congruent and complementary. Scientific knowledge confirms the mutuality of God's creation and God's revelation in Scripture.

The objective of this book is to awaken sleeping and slumbering mankind; men, women and children, and jolt them into the reality of the dynamic and loving God. The objective is to have every person open their eyes, ears, mind, heart and awareness to see the wonders of what God is doing all around us in his creation, and what God is saying to us as individuals, families, communities, peoples and nations through his revelation. It is a monumental tragedy for any person, group or nation to live on the earth and fail to see the glory of God, to hear and learn of God's will for our individual and collective lives. What a tragedy to live on the earth for years and fail to see the visible glory of God and to hear the audible words of God. Writing this book will be worthwhile if one person awakes and sees the glory of God in God's creation and hears God's word from God's perpetual revelation. "But seek ye first the kingdom of God, and his righteousness; and all these things shall be added unto you." (Matthew 6:33).

The glaring revelation of God in his creation, the Holy Bible and in Jesus Christ can be missed only through a radically self-imposed blindness, deafness, ignorance and willful denial. If you should miss seeing and experiencing the revelation of God's glory during your lifetime, you will have missed the greatest thing of all!

ACKNOWLEDGEMENTS

Thanks be to the loving and merciful God of Jesus Christ for leading and sustaining me on my journey of life. It is not possible to name the numerous persons and situations that influenced my life that led me to write this volume. Only a very few will be mentioned to give a kind of chronology and perspective on from whence I have come by faith.

I was fortunate to have loving parents and family. I am grateful. My educational experience provided me with loving classmates and inspiring teachers from elementary school and middle school in Notasulga, Alabama through Tuskegee Institute High School in Tuskegee, Alabama. It was Lyda M. Yette, my math and science teacher in high school who helped me to recognize that I had good mental ability.

I am eternally grateful to Macedonia Baptist Church in Notasulga, Alabama, where I accepted Christ as my Lord and Savior as a child and was later licensed and ordained to preach the gospel. Several years ago, the State of Alabama placed a plaque in front of Macedonia Baptist Church in honor of Zora Neal Hurston for her literary accomplishments.

It was Rev. Lucius M. Tobin, Professor of Religion at Morehouse College, along with Dr. Benjamin E. Mays, President of Morehouse, who inspired me to study and to appreciate the understanding of our growing culture crisis in America. I am still proud of the honor that Morehouse bestowed upon me the year I graduated. I was chosen as the

Most Outstanding Student in Religion, delivered the Senior Sermon and the recipient of The Benjamin E. Mays Debating Prize.

It was a joy and labor of love to have served as Director of Youth Christian Education and Assistant Minister to The Rev. William H. Borders, Sr., Pastor of Wheat Street Baptist Church for more than 20 years. It was also my honor to serve one year as Interim Pastor of Wheat Street Baptist Church of Atlanta, Georgia. It was my privilege to work with many youth at Wheat Street who became ministers and pastors of the gospel. Among them are, Rev. Ted Benson, Rev. Albert E. Love, Rev. Hoke L. Smith, Rev. Dr. William H. Robinson, Rev. Charles Bronner, Rev. Nathaniel Bronner, Rev. Stanley Bronner and Bishop Dale Bronner. Also, the matriarch of the Bronner family, Mrs. Robbie Bronner, provided great support for the Sunday School, Youth Division and the Community Bus Ministry of the Wheat Street Baptist Church. Deacon and Mrs. Charles Christian and their three sons were diligent in providing professional video recordings of the Wheat Street Worship Service Television Ministry.

My pursuit of graduate study brought me in contact with many wonderful, committed students to worthy causes and the ministry as well as inspirational instructors. I pay tribute to Dr. Tilman Cothran of Atlanta University, Dr. Francis Bridges of Georgia State University and Dr. Edward Wimberly and Dr. Carolyn McCrary of ITC (Interdenominational Theological Center) in Atlanta, Georgia.

I also had the privilege of being an adjunct Instructor at ITC for six years where I taught twelve courses in the Continuing Education Extension Program. Many of my students graduated from ITC with a Certificate of Theology. Through the interaction and fellowship with these ITC students, I incorporated two organizations through the State of Georgia. They are The Christian Association of Public Theologians and The Christian Institute of Public Theology.

I am grateful for and indebted to many of my students and associates who have served as board members, leaders and supporters of these two organizations. CAPT (Christian Association of Public Theologians) has concluded 8 annual conferences. Thanks to Rev. Melvin Ware, Elder Willie Tuggle III, Mrs. Alma Simmons, Min. Marleesha Carmichael, Min. Thomas Luke, Min. of Music Karen Webb Allen, Rev. Dorie Tuggle, Min. of Music Rodney Allen, Min. Donnie Bell, Min. Gloria Ross, Rev. Charles Styles, Dr. Abraham Davis, Dr. Robert Perdue, Dr. Robert Franklin and many others associated with CAPT.

I am indebted to many of my clients and colleagues in the fields of mental health and criminal justice. I am grateful to be the chair for clergy training with the Concerned Black Clergy of Atlanta. Thanks to Dr. Robert Cobble and Rev. Frank Brown, Presidents of CBC (Concerned Black Clergy) and other members of CBC.

The persons who have been significant support for me in this broad range of ministry, have been the members and ministers of Foundation Community Church at Summerset

Assisted Living Community. Thanks to my daughter, Karen Webb Allen and her husband Rodney Allen, as ministers of music. Thanks to Dr. Abraham Davis, Sunday School teacher and musical vocalist. Thanks to these three preaching and teaching ministers who have lightened my burdens at the church significantly: Minister Marleesha Carmichael, Minister Thomas Luke and Minister Gloria Ross. Appreciation is extended to the great spirit and the great musical talent of Ozzie Ross, Jr. and his grandmother, Mae Frances Luke. Thanks to Briana Arnold, the poetist. Thanks to all the faith members for your service and dedication. Thanks to Rev. Thomas Ball for his 5 years of service at the Foundation.

Extraordinary thanks to my wife, Wilma and my daughter, Karen, who have been; not only supportive but sacrificial, in support of this husband and this father, who has been caught up in the ministry of Christ for over 50 years. It has required much sacrifice on their part. I am confident that God has a crown of Glory for all who endure to the end.

Thanks to P.J. Davenport for her technological skills in the typing and organization of this manuscript. Thanks to all persons, known and unknown, who have contributed to this literary production- Ezekiel Saw the Wheel-Can You See the Cross?

Willie J. Webb
Author

CHAPTER 1

INTRODUCTION

This book is about the universality of the Bible and its message for all human beings for all time. Ezekiel Saw the Wheel—Can You See the Cross? was chosen as the title because of the universality of the wheel and the universality of the cross. This book will explore and illustrate the relationship between the wheel and the cross. This book reveals or makes clear the commonality of God's universal creation with the Bible. The vast visible evidence of God's creation is self-evident. It was intended for man to witness existence and God's creation. (In this book, MAN is used generically, to be inclusive of women and humanity.) It is amazing that as the Bible is studied with faith and spiritual insight, it becomes clear that the God of universal creation is the same God that is revealed in Scripture, the Bible.

There is clear evidence that the author of the Bible, beginning with the book of Genesis knew about globalism or the global earth before primitive people had any exposure to understand the global concept of the earth. Primitive man was confined to small areas villages or communities for thousands of years before they learned to make boats and ships and navigate directions.

However, there are 935 references to the earth in the Bible.

There are 751 references to the earth in the Old Testament. There are 184 references to the earth in the New Testament. Genesis has 121 references to the earth. The Book of Psalms has 141 references to the earth. Isiah has 101 references to the planet. Jeremiah 59, and Job has 50 references to the earth. In the New Testament, the five books with the highest number of references to the earth are Revelation 79, Matthew 27, Acts 18, Luke 17 and Mark 9.

Job makes a most astounding statement about the earth in (Job 26:7). How could Job have known that the earth was suspended in space three thousand years ago? The scientist learned that the earth was suspended in space in about the 16 century A.D. during the time of Copernicus. Job also refers to God as he who is able, "to shake the earth out of her place" (Job 9:6), and which "make Arcturus, Orion, and Pleiades, and the Chambers of the south (Job 9:9)." These quotations from the book of Job are clear indications that these references are to the universal all-powerful Creator God. These are not references to polytheistic gods or any earthly or local gods with the lowercase g. Job refers to the one monotheistic God who created the heavens and the earth. Job gives his concept of God and the universe when raises this question, "Is not God in the height of heaven? and behold the height of the stars, how high they are!" (Job 22:12). Job indicates man's relationship to the earth when he says, "all flesh shall perish together, and man shall turn again unto dust." (Job 34:15).

Isaiah, an 8TH century Hebrew prophet, reiterates Job when Isaiah says, " therefore, I will shake the heavens, and the earth shall remove out of her place." (Isaiah 13:13). Isaiah advances the thought of the movability of the earth 2400 years before science made that discovery through a theory of Nicolaus Copernicus in 1543 A.D. Isaiah predates Ptolemy (150 A.D.) approximately 800 years. There are other prophets, Joel 3:16, and Haggai 2:6, who allude to God shaking the heavens and the earth.

It is important to make note of this because it is not conceivable that primitive minds with naturally limited exposure and mobility could conceive of the earth being moved or shaken out of its place. This is a modern global concept. It is also noted worthy to mention that Abraham, Moses, David and the 8TH century Hebrew prophets predate the Greek philosophers in 500-300 B.C. The Greeks were known for knowledge. However, as you read Ezekiel Saw the Wheel, you see that the knowledge of the Bible surpasses the knowledge of the Greeks regarding the earth and man's moral and ethical relationship with man and God.

The theory of evolution is a recent theory in history that seems to persist in spite of its flaws and shortcomings. The Theory of Evolution is based on Charles Darwin's Origin of Species in 1859 A.D. The theory advances the idea that human life evolved from lower forms of life. No solid evidence has been found to confirm the validity of this theory. However, the theory of evolution is being taught in the school systems. Most public schools do not allow the Bible to be taught. The educational contrast between teaching the theory of evolution and the factual creationism of the Bible is very revealing.

One of the reasons Ezekiel Saw the Wheel is so important, is because it illustrates in graphic forms the objective validity of Biblical creationism as well as ID (Intelligent Design) which is found in the Bible and everywhere visible throughout the universe. The knowledge and scientific tools exist now to verify and validate the facts and truth of creationism and Intelligent Design.

Creationism and Intelligent Design are not secretive. They are not hidden or concealed. They are open before the world. God the Creator has created matter in at least three identifiable forms. Matter can be observed in solid, liquid and gaseous forms. Who can reasonably or logically dispute or contest the facts of the matter? Matter has also been divided into categories of organic and inorganic substances and a large body of classifications. Even matter itself is intelligently designed. The universe is cosmological (ordered) and not chaos.

What is the point? The point is, since God's creation is so self-evident; and that the truth of the Bible has been validated by the rigorous tests of centuries of time and human circumstance; all people everywhere ought to accept this truth, believe it, teach it and live it. Human life and human survival depend on accepting the reality and truth revealed by God.

The knowledge of creation, the Creator and the revelation of the truth of Scripture supersede all other knowledge. It is the knowledge above all knowledge and the name above every name. It is inescapable. Rejecting this knowledge of God is an act of retreating into an unreal world of fantasy. Worse than the retreat from the truth and reality, it is also rebellion against God. When creatures rebel against their Creator, it is a serious matter. Rebellion against God by Israel was the circumstance that brought about the appearance of the wheels (Ezekiel 1:16).

Ezekiel Saw the Wheel is chosen to portray some revelations of God and some revelations of the Cross. The wheel is among the greatest inventions of man. The wheel is round as the celestial bodies of the universe are round-shaped. The wheel is associated with spinning, turning, rolling, revolving, traveling and transporting. Wheel in the singular is used 14 times in the Bible. Wheel is used seven times in the book of Ezekiel. The plural of wheel (wheels) is used 33 times in the Bible. It is used 22 times in Ezekiel.

The number 4 is a significant number in connection with the wheels that Ezekiel saw. The number 4 is used 319 times in the Bible and 47 times in the book of Ezekiel. The earth and the cross have 4 primary directions. They are north, south, east and west. The Bible refers to the four winds and the four corners of the earth, which signify directions. Again, this emphasizes the global emphasis of the Bible regarding the earth.

In considering directions, the Bible has 131 references to the direction east. Ezekiel has 55 of the 131 references to the east. The Bible has 131 references to the direction north.

Ezekiel has 40 of the 131 references to North. (More than any other single book in the Bible.) Ezekiel has 25 of 69 references to the direction west in the Bible. Ezekiel has 29 of 61 references to the direction south in the Bible. Ezekiel describes the wheels and the universal direction for travel and movement.

Every wheel has 360 degrees. The 360 degrees make a circle with 4 right angles. The four ninety-degree angles make a cross. Every wheel constitutes a circle with a cross or crosses within. It is amazing how round balanced wheels make for a smooth spin or ride with minimum friction.

It is interesting to notice that the creatures and the wheels that Ezekiel saw came out of a whirlwind (Ezekiel 1:4). This whirling wind further perpetuates the turning and revolving characteristics of celestial bodies and universal principles. The earth spins at a rate of over 1,000 miles per hour. The Earth travels around the sun at the rate of 66,600 miles per hour (World Book Encyclopedia). Scientist also says that the Solar System revolves around the Milky Way Galaxy.

Ezekiel Saw the Wheel teaches significant lessons. The wheel is designed for a dynamic purpose. The function of the wheel is driven by a dynamic purpose with superior intelligence. The various wheels presented in this work give insight into universal principles designed by the Creator. At the heart, core and center of the wheel will be found the cross. This cross is the wheel in the middle of the wheel. Ezekiel says the spirit is in the wheels (Ezekiel 1:20).

The center of the wheel has a generating power. The central core of celestial bodies produces a gravitational force. What is at the core of this spherical-shaped earth that holds solids, liquids (including rivers and oceans that cover 70% of the earth's surface) and gases on the surface of the earth? The Bible declares that the creatures and the wheels that Ezekiel saw were a manifestation of the "appearance of the likeness of the glory of the Lord." (Ezekiel 1:28). God revealed this manifestation of his glory to show Israel that a prophet had been among them (Ezekiel 2:5).

Ezekiel Saw the Wheel-Can You See the Cross, is written to show the invincible reality of God through God's creation of the heavens and the earth, and God's revelation through the Bible and in Jesus Christ. The reality of God's creation and Biblical revelations are illustrated in this volume through religion, art, law and science. The centrality and the universality of the cross will be revealed in the expressions of religion, art, law and science. The horizontal and vertical dimensions of the Cross are a recurring theme that runs through this book.

The message that was given to Ezekiel for Israel on the day when Ezekiel saw the wheel, is the same message that is delivered to America and other nations in this, "impudent." And. "rebellious." Twenty-first century.

Willie James Webb

CHAPTER 2

THE VERTICAL DIMENSION OF SALVATION

The vertical dimension of the cross is significant for many reasons. One reason is that it transcends, rises above and supersedes the horizontal dimension. The horizontal dimension is on the secular level. The secular level is confined to the social affairs of the world. The secular world has no ambition or aspiration to connect with God above. For the most part, the horizontal secular world denies the existence or the need to establish a spiritual connection and upreach to God. This is not intended to be a condemnation of secularism or the human horizontal dimension. The point is to show the significant limitation of the earth-bound horizontal dimension.

This earth-bound or worldly secularism limits our thinking, distorts reality and perpetuates unsound values, ideologies and doctrines. The distortion of reality and acceptance of unsound values and ideologies contribute to mental and spiritual illness. The mental and spiritual illnesses translate into making a sick society and a sick culture. The sickness is compounded and exacerbated by bad social policies, unjust laws and misguided leaders and public officials.

A case in point illustrates the erroneous thinking and actions of persons confined to secular decisions on the horizontal plane with no regard for the vertical dimension of the cross. Fox News reported on December 13, 2013, that a Federal U.S. District Judge, Larry Burns, ordered that the 40-plus foot War Memorial Cross on San Diego Mountain in California be removed because it represents a religious symbol and it is located on public property. The Cross was placed on San Diego Mountain in 1952 to honor the war-dead soldiers. The ACLU and the non-Christian groups that brought the suit celebrated the U.S. District Judge's decision to remove the cross. However, Defense Attorney Bruce Bailey expressed plans to appeal the case to the Supreme Court.

It is quite apparent that persons who brought the War Memorial Cross on San Diego Mountain Suit to Federal Court, their ACLU representatives and sympathizers have the limited and distorted thinking that was alluded to earlier. The fact and the overwhelming evidence that the Cross is a universal symbol and not limited to religion eludes them. It eludes them because of their secular ideas, values, doctrines and ideologies. How could a solitary Cross on a mountain, established in 1952 to honor the U.S. war dead be offensive to any American, even if they are not patriotic? It would seem that there would be other structures, buildings and environmental hazards and dangers that would merit targeting for demolition and court litigation. How safe are our bridges and tunnels? How safe are our communities from the levies and dams during floods? How safe are the structures of our homes, schools and countless other structures and buildings in the community in the face of tornadoes, hurricanes, earthquakes, terroristic attacks and other unanticipated natural and manmade disasters? We live at a time in history when reasonable people must at the least, acknowledge with existing hostilities and technological capabilities that nuclear warfare is within prospective possibilities.

I believe that the point has been made that possible harm from the War Memorial Cross on the San Diego Mountain in California, pales into insignificance when compared to the other real dangers in American society. Somehow, secular thinking causes us to shut out significant reality and major in minors and side issues.

The vertical and spiritual dimension of the cross exposes those who embrace its, knowledge from above. It is knowledge from above where we get sound ethical values, doctrines and truth. Those who restrict themselves to the horizontal secular values, become, inescapably, tainted, influenced or socialized with the isms of the world. Hardly anyone is exempt from being influenced by these isms of the world. However, there is a way to overcome the imprisonment of the isms of the world. But first, we will list some basic isms of the world. They will be placed in two categories. One category is the isms associated with groups of people. The second category is associated with individual isms.

The knowledge from above references the revelatory knowledge found in the Old Testament and the New Testament of the Bible. Those who have given serious theological study of the Bible conclude that the collection of the 66 canonized books of the Bible contains universal truths, principles and ethics that apply to all mankind. Jesus Christ is the most widely known and the most celebrated person of all history for two thousand years. His uniqueness has not been repeated after two thousand years. The Bible teaches that the Bible contains the authoritative word of God. Secularism attempts to exclude the Bible and Jesus Christ from the culture and public life.

To the extent that biblical knowledge is excluded from the American culture and public life; to the same extent certain ideological isms on the secular level become influential belief systems devoid of God. Secularism aims for a Godless society. Its aim is for an exclusively horizontal dimension. It does not wish to be reminded of the horizontal and vertical dimensions of the cross. There is increased energy used to get the cross and Christ out of culture. Since human beings have an inherent worship capacity, they will create idol gods to worship. The idol gods are false gods. The idol god worshippers create confusion and havoc for themselves and society. There is no salvation in the idol gods. There is no lasting spiritual or human fulfillment by the idol gods.

However, those persons who hate the Cross and Christ continue to create their idol gods to the detriment of themselves and society. The isms that people create can, and often do, become idol gods. The primary problem with the idol god is that it is false and limited. The isms and the idol gods are too small to accommodate the wholeness of human life. These isms and false gods are often accompanied by certain ideologies that are exclusive, discriminatory and divisive. Oftentimes, the idol worshippers take on an ideological identification that associates them with the particular ism. The ideologies can cause them to become extremist, radical and even violent. People who are not guided by the light and knowledge from the vertical dimension of the cross can become toxic, explosive and misguided cannons of destruction.

The following is a list of twelve isms and ideologies that exist in American society. These isms are associated predominantly with groups. This is not an exhaustive list. This list is used as an example of many groups that do not necessarily have any sacred or spiritual connection from above. However, they can be potent influences in the secular realm of society:

1. Sectarianism
2. Cultism
3. Classism
4. Racism
5. Partisanism
6. Nationalism
7. Socialism
8. Communism

9. Capitalism
10. Religionism
11. Tribalism
12. Sexism

These isms existing on a horizontal secular plane are not necessarily bad within themselves. There can be many positive things about each listed ism. It is when they become ideological idol gods and reject God with the Capital G that they become problematic. Whenever any person or group assume the posture that they can get along without God or that they are independent of God, they have denied or disconnected with ultimate reality and truth.

True religion requires vertical preaching to God and horizontal outreach to mankind. The cross has those two dimensions. This does not just apply to people who identify themselves as Christians. It applies to everyone who claims to have true religion. Jesus confirms this truth by quoting the Great Commandment of the law: "You shall love the Lord your God, with all your heart, mind, soul and strength. And you shall love your neighbor as yourself."

Let every soul be subject unto the higher powers. For there is no power but of God: the powers that be are ordained of God. (Romans 13:1).

The message in the Judeo-Christian Bible has jurisdiction over every soul. No one is outside of the jurisdiction of the God of Adam, Abraham, Isaac, Jacob, Jesus and all the descendants of humanity. He has made of one blood all nations of men for to dwell on all the face of the earth and has determined the times before appointed, and the bounds of their habitation (Acts 17:26). The cross is inclusive of all humanity because it has a circumference of 360° which makes an inclusive circle.

Problems of the Isms

The isms lack the quality of being inclusive and universal. They are characterized by being provincial, limited, self-centered and exclusive. The limited and self-serving focus of the isms keeps them secularly and horizontally bound. The limited secular bondage precludes the isms from a transcendent rescue from above. All persons restricted to the horizontal dimension have no vertical dimension to appeal to. Since man has a built-in spiritual capacity from God, he becomes unbalanced when that capacity is not filled or satisfied with spiritual nourishment and God's word from above. Therefore, certain deficits or spiritual and mental illnesses begin to occur. These spiritual, mental illnesses and personal imbalances begin to impair judgment and healthy decision making. They become detached from the wholeness of social reality and become an all-consuming fictional unreality of their own making.

The isms do not have to be reality based. Often, they deny reality. A belief in an ideology does not require facts or validated reality or truth. However, in their distorted and exaggerated thinking, the fictions become reality to them.

And as W.I. Thomas, sociologist, explains the definition of the situation, states that, "when men define situations as real, though they be false in fact, they are real in their consequences."

When leaders and public officials make laws and influence public policy, it is important to know what isms are motivating and driving them. It is dangerous for the society when leaders make decisions based on the secular based horizontal isms without regard to the vertical reality of God. Leaders are rising up and public officials are being put in office and leadership positions daily without our knowing what particular isms they embrace. The possible tragic and harmful consequences are self-evident. Some isms blind, limit, exclude, circumscribe, steal, persecute and destroy. Those isms do a wide range of harm. The severity ranges from mild, to the radical and the extreme. Are your leaders guided by the Light of Christ or the darkness of the secular world?

There is some good news and there is some bad news. I will give you the bad news first. Because of the technological capabilities for massive destruction, if we fail to reverse this engulfing horizontal darkness in America and the world, human life will be destroyed. The idol worship, the denial of God's word in the Bible and the antichrist and the anti-cross spirits have already set the inhabitants of the earth on a course of destruction. The prospect of Dooms Day is looming in the horizon. This bad news is getting dangerously worse because of disobedience and rebellion against a loving God who sacrificed his Son on the Cross for the salvation of the world. The rejection of God and his Christ triggers damnation and self-destruction.

The good news is that while there is life and a little time is left, the march to Dooms Day and destruction can be turned around. This turning around is linked to man's response to the revelations in the cross and of the cross. Secular minded leadership poses the great danger to the destruction of humanity on the planet earth. Leadership that is anti-God or indifferent to God or embrace the secular idol gods, mislead nations to destruction. These kind of leaders do not rise to political power on their own. They do not get there through a vacuum. They are voted and supported into leadership and public office by the populous, bureaucratic and political power structures. In a nation such as America, most of the population do not participate in the political process. Most Americans are not interested enough to be sufficiently informed about the candidates for public office to vote intelligently. Most of the voters know very little about the individuals they vote into public office as well as other leadership positions in the community.

There is a pattern and a predictable trend that the more secularism invades and pervades society the less the people know about their leaders and the less responsibility most people take for their leadership and the less they care about who leads. In spite of the quantitative, educational and technological advances in America, there is evidence that a qualitative dumbing down is taking place. This qualitative dumbing down is connected to the vertical dimension of the cross. There is a growing gross neglect of the traditional, ethical, moral, historical and spiritual values and principles handed down in the Judeo-Christian Bible. America was built on the Judeo-Christian values. It is inconceivable that America can survive without its foundation of Judeo-Christian values.

At this time in history these revelatory values from God above are being ignored, disobeyed and eroded in the American society. They are not just being eroded, these sacred values and traditions are being trampled on. On December 23, 2013, Fox News reported that soldiers at Camp Shelby were forbidden to use the word Christian at an annual Christmas sports event. Also, in South Alabama there was a group of men, who happen to have been black, dressed as women, prancing down the street in majorette style, to the shock and dismay of parents who brought their children to watch the parade. There are schools that are removing the word "Christ" out of the Christmas Carol, <u>Silent Night</u>. There are many instances where Nativity scenes are not allowed. There are instances where schools are using unisex bathrooms to accommodate the students who are said to be gay. Instances were reported by Fox News where the VA (Veterans Administration) returned cards addressed to veteran patients because the cards had, so called, Christian religious references. This outrageous war against Christians has escalated significantly in the past four years. The Christmas spirit has brought more joy and more peace to the world than any other spirit or event for 2000 years. Those spirits that are offended by the Christmas Spirit are the greatest offenders of all to peace, goodwill and humanity. Initiatives are being taken to counteract the war on Christmas and the cross. Republican Congressman has introduced a Saving Christmas Bill that will protect the Biblical references and traditions associated with Christmas.

By way of footnote, and in view of the War on Christmas and Christ, the guardians of truth and the Church must be extra vigilant in the compilation and the distribution of information and knowledge to all educational institutions as well as to the public at large. The guardians of truth must monitor the validity, appropriateness and truthfulness of disseminated knowledge from pre-kindergarten through the university.

Serious U.S. Cultural Meltdown

There is a distinct correlation between the decline of the sacred Judeo-Christian values and the rise of secularism in conjunction with the ethical, moral and spiritual decay in the American culture. From its earliest beginnings from the thirteen colonies in the early 1600s to about 1970 America was a predominantly Christian country. The majority of the Americans who claimed a religious affiliation identified themselves as Protestants, Catholics and Jews during this 360 years of American history. Over 80% of the population identified themselves as Christians. The past 50 years have brought about tumultuous social changes with a significant reduction in the percentage of Americans who identify themselves as Christians.

This general religious identification of predominant Christian maintained itself during the Revolutionary War, African American enslavement, the Civil War, World War 1, World War II, Korean and Vietnam Wars and the Civil Rights Movement of the 1960s. Without taking the time to analyze and interpret the causal factors that brought about the moral decay and meltdown of ethical and spiritual values in America, I will simply list contributing factors for future consideration.

1. There were deaths and assassinations of significant leaders, including President Kennedy and Dr. Martin L. King, Jr. associated with Civil Rights in the 1960s.

2. There was inadequate preparation, acceptance and implementation of the 1964 Civil Rights Laws to achieve desegregation and integration.

3. There was inadequate preparation for the racial integration of the public schools and public accommodations in the 1960s and 1970s.

4. There was hardly any special preparation for over 50 million immigrants who came to America between 1970 and 2013.

5. Americans were severely traumatized by the 911 Terror attack that destroyed the World Trade Center Towers in New York City, damaged the Pentagon and took the lives of over 3000 Americans on September 11, 2001.

6. The Iraq and the Afghanistan Wars put a severe strain on the U.S. Treasury and brought about the death of over four thousand soldiers and injuries to additional thousands. Remnants of the war continue.

7. The Mortgage Foreclosure Crisis culminating in 2008 did great damage to millions of home ownership investors along with the damage to the American economy.

8. The massive oil spill in the gulf did great damage to the environment, fishing and oil industry and the escalation of gas prices at the pumps.

9. The shutdown of the government, sequestration, high unemployment, the ongoing controversies regarding gay rights, same sex marriage and the Affordable Healthcare Act, the NSA (National Security Agency) secret electronic surveillance, recording and storage of Americans' electronic communications.

10. The ongoing concerns about Iran's ambition to develop nuclear weapons and delivery systems, the civil wars in Syria, Egypt and Libya and concerns about Israel's war posture and defense capabilities.

11. The American government and American society are very divided between democrats and republicans, religions and races, liberals and conservatives regarding immigration, taxation, education, homeland security, energy resources, and the political electoral and appointment processes.

12. Crime, the criminal justice and judicial systems are ongoing problems and concerns. Many Americans experience violations of their person, human rights and property rights. Most feel that there is not equity, remedy or justice to be found in the judicial system. The Trevon Martin murder by Zimmerman is a case in point.

The above enumerations are some factors that contribute to the very serious ethical and moral meltdown in American society.

Critical U.S. Cultural Meltdown

The very foundation of America is being eroded. The anchor institutions, the survival values, the sound doctrines and the guiding principles are deteriorating and disintegrating at a rapid rate.

The areas of corrosion and the corresponding meltdown are illustrated below:

Areas	Meltdown Characteristics
1. Education and Knowledge	Illiteracy, Ignorance, Darkness
2. Truth and Understanding	Lies, Fiction and Confusion
3. Intelligence and Wisdom	Stupidity, Irresponsible, Foolishness

4. Professionalism and Ethics	Rudeness, Incompetence, Fraudulent
5. Religion and Morality	Idolatry, Immorality, Criminality
6. Marriage and Family	Illicit Unions, Sacrilegious Relationships
7. Church and School	Secularism, Greed, Undisciplined Assemblies
8. Government and Law	Chaotic Arbitrary Decisions Conflicting Laws
9. Hospitals and Healthcare	Morbidity, Pathology, Death
10. Art and Science	Unbalanced, Misused, Misdirected
11. Business and Industry	Greed, Slothful, Inefficient Waste
12. Freedom and Justice	Bondage, Exploitation, Destruction

The meltdown is the lethal reversal of the supports for human life, civilized community living and the obedience to the will of God through God's commandments in the Bible. God's authoritative law has been handed down from above. Jesus Christ has come from God above with the way, the truth, the life, the light, and eternal salvation for mankind. The meltdown is happening because of the violation of God's laws and the rejection of Jesus Christ. The meltdown is happening because the vertical dimension of the cross is being ignored and rejected. The horizontal and vertical dimensions of the cross are the standards of balance set by God. When they are violated, the meltdown begins.

Aids for Reversing the Meltdown

The quality of American leadership from the National level to the State and local levels is primarily responsible for the American cultural meltdown. The process of electing and appointing leadership in America is arbitrary, irresponsible, ineffective and dangerous. There are no adequate qualifying standards for elective office. The elected leadership and appointed officials of the government are the ones who influence public opinions, make the laws, interpret the laws and enforce the laws. The general population does not know the true identification of their official leaders. They do not know them because they (the people) have not established credible thought-out standards and qualifications for their leaders and public officials. With such an arbitrary haphazard selection leadership process, it is conceivable that the people may vote their worst enemies into leadership.

The Statue of Liberty-on-Liberty Island in New York Harbor expresses the character and exceptionality of America. The Statue was given to America by the people of France on July 4, 1884. It was dedicated on October 28, 1886. The Statue's primary structure is held by four vertical iron beams with horizontal and diagonal iron beams. The crown that Liberty wears has seven spikes to represent the seven seas and the seven continents. At the feet of Liberty is a broken chain. In her right hand is a glowing torch. The statue's complete name is, "Liberty Enlightening the World." The base of the statue is enclosed with a wall-shaped star on a twelve-acre plot of land. The statue is an expression of the Americans (predominately Christian) inviting immigrants from all over the world.

Since 1884 (129 years later) the world has come to America with its cultural diversity, religious pluralism and internationalism in a democratic form of U.S. government. This accumulated diversity and pluralism contain a multiplicity of isms, ideologies, customs and traditions. Many of cultural differences are alien and foreign to the principles and traditions of America. This raises some critical questions that should have been asked and answered a hundred years ago: What are the ethical, moral, spiritual and socioeconomic political values that define the character of America? What are the specific moral, ethical, spiritual and socio-economic-political principles and values that will be used to guide America based on America's character and purpose? How can leaders and public officials be elected, appointed and be recognized as bonafide qualified leaders and officials with assurance that they represent the core values and the guiding principles of America? How can equitable codes of ethics and qualifications be developed and legislated into law to assure Americans and the nation that their leaders and public officials are leading and representing America with optimum competence, responsibility, accountability and patriotism?

The true Americans must raise the question and also answer the question: What individual Americans are best suited to lead America's institutions and government? The answer to this question will, hopefully, require serious thought and a well-written out job description for all candidates for public office before they get into the political race and before they get appointed to public office. This applies to all candidates for public office, including the office of the U.S. president and all other public offices from the federal to the state and local levels. A thorough vetting of all candidates must be required before they qualify to run for public office. American citizens must be informed about who the candidates are and what they stand for according to their ultimate belief systems. The qualification for public office in America is archaic and oblivious to the ideological, heterogeneous and technological realities of the Twenty-First century.

Many unsuitable candidates are getting public office and leadership positions because of lax standards and inadequate code of ethics. As a minimum, candidates for public office and leadership must have a sound and safe religious ideological philosophy that is compatible with the established religious ideological philosophy of the Nation (America) and the predominant historical National indigenous population. This is inclusive of a universal religious and philosophical inclusive sound doctrine for all people. The candidate must not have provincial sectarian, cultic, partisan or similar belief systems that deny the equality of any human beings or violate the unalienable rights endowed by the Creator. The candidate must be free of criminal records, mental, emotional and spiritual disorders and incapacities. The candidate must be free of drug abuse (including alcohol) dependence and other addictive disorders. It is essential that candidates for public office and leadership positions be qualified and mentally and spiritually healthy. Sick heads and spirits make sick bodies and sick societies and bring destruction to nations.

In an effort to determine the mental and ideological fitness for healthy, effective and positive leadership, the Christian Institute of Public Theology has developed an ism rating scale. This scale is not exhaustive. It contains 24 isms that can blind, limit, exclude, circumscribe and cause harm.

A Diagnostic Evaluation Instrument for Human Heterogeneous Fitness and Leadership Capability

THE ISM RATING SCALE

Classification	The ISM	Severity	Total
1.	Racism	0 1 2 3 4	
2.	Classism	0 1 2 3 4	
3.	Ethnocentrism	0 1 2 3 4	
4.	Elitism	0 1 2 3 4	
5.	Masochism	0 1 2 3 4	
6.	Tribalism	0 1 2 3 4	
7.	Sectarianism	0 1 2 3 4	
8.	Cultism	0 1 2 3 4	
9.	Partisanism	0 1 2 3 4	
10.	Asceticism	0 1 2 3 4	
11.	Narcissism	0 1 2 3 4	
12.	Nepotism	0 1 2 3 4	
13.	Secularism	0 1 2 3 4	
14.	Materialism	0 1 2 3 4	
15.	Agnosticism	0 1 2 3 4	
16.	Nihilism	0 1 2 3 4	
17.	Atheism	0 1 2 3 4	
18.	Egotism	0 1 2 3 4	
19.	Sadism	0 1 2 3 4	
20.	Fanaticism	0 1 2 3 4	
21.	Heathenism	0 1 2 3 4	
22.	Stoicism	0 1 2 3 4	
23.	Cynicism	0 1 2 3 4	
24.	Infantilism	0 1 2 3 4	

Total Severity

0= none   1= mild   2= moderate 3= severe 4= extreme

Name of Evaluator: Date:

Summary of the ISM Rating Scale

Human nature is susceptible to all of the isms listed above. There can be serious problems associated with each one of them. Many persons are influenced adversely by many of the isms listed above. Individuals may have these biases and subjective perceptions to the extent that their judgment, decision-making and leadership ability may be seriously and detrimentally impaired. It is unfortunate and in many instances, tragic, that most people do not evolve beyond or transcend the above-listed isms. This poses a serious problem and challenges for education and leadership in our global society. What are the qualifications for competent teachers, ministers, public servants and leaders in a global heterogeneous society? In addition to ism rating scales, it is now necessary to develop more instruments to evaluate, assess and determine the spiritual and ideological identities of individuals who are in the society with a potential of doing harm due to their particular spiritual and ideological ismatisms.

The Christian Institute of Public Theology, Inc.

CIPT (The Christian Institute of Public Theology is in the process of developing a DSM (Diagnostic Statistical Manual) for spiritual disorders. This manual is being developed similarly to the DSMV for mental disorders that was published by the APA (American Psychiatric Association) for mental disorders. The Bible, itself, is the primary source for spiritual disorders. There is sufficient information for developing a diagnostic instrument to assess spiritual disorders as well as spiritual injuries.

The following two instruments are not intended to be comprehensive or exhaustive. They are basic and practical assessments for spiritual disorders and spiritual injuries. They can be used by professionally trained certified or licensed mental health and spiritual health professionals. The twenty-four categories are basic categories and are not inclusive of all injuries or disorders that exist. It would be ideal for professionally recognized theological seminaries, Law Schools and medical schools to combine their academic knowledge to produce a diagnostic statistical manual encompassing mental and spiritual health for the good, order and ethical function of a healthy society. America has outstanding capable medical, law and theological schools.

ASSESSMENT FOR SPIRITUAL INJURIES

Injury	Severity	Duration	Last Occurrence
1. Anger			
2. Anxiety			
3. Bitterness			
4. Confusion			
5. Demoralization			
6. Despair			
7. Disbelief			
8. Discouraged			
9. Distressed			
10. Doubtful			
11. Fearful			
12. Grief			
13. Guilt			
14. Hopelessness			
15. Infuriation			
16. Indignant			
17. Intimidation			
18. Disoriented			
19. Rage			
20. Resentment			
21. Revengeful			
22. Sadness			
23. Sorrow			
24. Shame			

Severity: Low, Mild, Severe _____

Duration: Length of time of injury _____

Last Effects: Date of Last Symptoms _____

Name of Evaluator: _____ Date: _____

The Assessment for Spiritual Injuries

The assessment of spiritual injuries can be helpful in getting a picture of how a person functions while enduring the stressful difficulties and misfortunes in their lives. It helps to learn about their strengths, temperaments, emotional maturity, motivations, values and commitments. It helps to learn things about the person's character that would not be revealed on the usual job applications and resumes. Currently, the information that is most needed from candidates for public office is left out.

The spiritual injuries listed on the assessment form are the kinds of injuries that can happen to anyone. Therefore, the idea of assessing for injuries of potential public office holders and leaders is not negative. It is positive to assure the citizens that their representatives and leaders are suitable and capable of doing the best job possible for the constituents and the community. Mental health, spiritual health, and ethical and professional health have been overlooked and minimized for much too long. The focus on the spiritual, moral, ethical and professional health of our public officials must take a top priority. In order to have and maintain a healthy society, it is mandatory that the leaders be healthy. The responsible representatives of the people must establish human health standards and qualifications for public officials and community leaders. The spiritually disordered leaders are more dangerous and damaging to society than the physically and mentally disordered leaders. Adolph Hitler is a case in point.

The more secular the American society becomes; the more at-risk America is for deterioration of survival values and destruction. The more secular the society becomes, the more blind and indifferent its members become to moral and spiritual values. We are rapidly approaching the "red line" of no return.

The following assessment is for Spiritual Disorders:

ASSESSMENT FOR SPIRITUAL DISORDERS

Disorder	Severity	Duration	Last Occurrence
1. Abuse			
2. Cruelty			
3. Deceitful			
4. Dishonesty			
5. Envious			
6. Evil			
7. Greed			
8. Hateful			
9. Idolatrous			
10. Iniquitous			
11. Irreverent			
12. Jealousy			
13. Malicious			
14. Pride (arrogant)			
15. Profane			
16. Sadistic			
17. Slothful			
18. Self-Centered			
19. Ungodly			
20. Unjust			
21. Unrighteousness			
22. Vindictive			
23. Vulgarity			
24. Wickedness			

<u>Evaluation Directions</u>

Severity: Low, Moderate, Extreme _____

Duration: Length of Time of Disorder _____

Last Occurrence: Date of Last Symptom _____

Name of Evaluator: _____ Date: _____

Evaluate Deficits for Leadership

All of the isms, the ism rating scale and the assessment for spiritual inquiries and the assessment for spiritual disorders have one thing in common. They exist, originate and operate on the horizontal secular level. They all are tainted, perverted or corrupted by negatives. A negative is a minus sign. The minus sign is the horizontal sign. The minus sign is a subtracting sign. It takes away from the whole. Continuous subtracting creates regressive deficits. Deficits do not give. Deficits take away.

Individuals with mental, emotional, ideological, professional and spiritual deficits are hardly suitable to represent and lead others. Somehow, the deficits within them as heads or leaders, create deficits within the body or the constituents that they lead. The isms are tainted with biases, subjectivity and exclusive ideologies. The listed twenty-four spiritual injuries along with the twenty-four spiritual disorders hinder the effective job performance of the public office holder or leader. All of these isms, spiritual injuries and spiritual disorders ought to be discovered before the candidate for political office is certified to run for office or appointed or otherwise be installed in the leadership position.

The purpose of this proposed evaluation for screening out unsuitable candidates and leaders for public office is to emphasize the seriousness of the problem and the urgency to make the correction in this damaging oversight. There is a trend for secular-minded or horizontal dimension people to start recruiting people with their particular isms, disorders and ideologies. This is very unhealthy and dangerous for the society. This is not meant to condemn secularism or the horizontal dimension of living. This is an effort to show the importance of the secular being balanced with the sacred. The Cross has a horizontal and vertical dimension. Secularism is anti-God and anti-Christ. It seems to perpetuate the deception that man can get along without God. Security and salvation exist only in God. Our ultimate help is from the vertical dimension. Our survival values are from the vertical dimension. Jesus stated that he came not to condemn the world, but to save the world. When men are left to their own devices they end up destroying themselves.

Human beings must have the guidance of righteousness, justice, light, truth, knowledge, wisdom and understanding. The right way is not arbitrary or random. God has set standards for right, true and just decisions. The right, true and just decision is in accord with the Will of God. The Will of God is revealed more clearly through the Bible and Jesus Christ than any other known sources.

It should be very obvious by now, that if the people we elect, appoint or follow, as public officials and leaders who do not have God, the Bible or Jesus Christ as their authority and standard for decision-making, our leadership is in arbitrary darkness. Test the spirits of your Candidate for leadership and public office, and see whether they have the spirit of God. The technology of the 21s century has made it too dangerous to elect, appoint, support or follow leaders who are not of the spirit of God, and who do not know the Will of God. While recognizing certain individual rights existing in a democratic form of government, common sense 101 suggests that it is foolish, irresponsible and insane to entrust leadership to disordered minds and iniquitous spirits.

Vertical Dimension Transformation

The Minus Sign

It is amazing that two simple straight lines can have such significant meaning and power. Those two lines of the cross have significant meanings when they are separate. They have an even greater significance when they are combined. The straight horizontal line is known as a minus sign in mathematics and a negative sign in science. It is an underline in English and art. It is a horizontal or across line when it is horizontal to the earth. It is also a hundred-eighty-degree angle in geometry. It is the secular dimension of the earth when it is devoid of God, heaven and religion. It is also known as a dash. A dash is a straight line that connects two related words or sentences. It is usually a dash that is used to measure the length of time from birth to death. In the construction industry, it is a leveler used to measure a flat surface. The minus sign also indicates subtraction. The minus sign indicates the line between east and west.

The one simple line of the minus sign has many uses and many symbolic meanings. Many good things can, and have happened on the horizontal level. God created the earth and all the inhabitants thereof. Moreover, God declared that his creation was good. However, man's continuing disobedience brought separation and alienation between God and man. But God's love for man caused God to send down a plumb line of lifeline in his Word and his Son, Jesus Christ.

God made provision by extending a vertical dimension from heaven above to connect with the horizontal dimension on the earth below to give a salvation option to live with God eternally.

It is unreasonable to think that man would be reaching up to God, had not God first reached down for man. The initiative to reach man was taken by God. From the vertical dimension, it was God's revelation down to man. From man's helpless and hopeless horizontal position from below, he looks up, seeking for and searching for God's revelation from above. Man's search was in response to God's prior revelation. God created the place, time, conditions and possibilities for man to reach up. When God gives wise men and humble men a star of hope, they go seeking and searching for the meaning of that star of hope.

Life Line from Above

The lifeline from above is God's vertical dimension to communicate to a man on the earth good tidings, great joy and good news. God's vertical lifeline is a line of communication, a line of connection and a line of rescue. It is that vertical line that connects and intersects with the horizontal dimension of man and makes a cross of salvation. This cross becomes a transformer and makes all things new. The minus sign becomes a plus sign. The negative sign becomes a positive sign. Subtraction is transformed into addition. The dash from birth to death is extended to eternity. The horizontal line that pointed from east to west now has a new dimension. This new vertical dimension points from the south below to the north above. It points from the earth below to God above. This single straight-line dimension has been transformed into two dimensions with four directions. These four directions constitute a 360-degree complete circle. The circle has become the round universal symbol of the celestial bodies of the creations. The circle has no beginning and no ending. The cross in the circle has become a wheel in the middle of a wheel.

A Wheel in the Middle of a Wheel

The Cross in the circle has become a wheel in the middle of a wheel. This is a moving wheel. It is a turning wheel. It is a revolving wheel. It is a direction wheel. It is a salvation wheel. It is a science wheel. It is an art wheel. It is a time wheel. It is a season wheel. It is a month of the year wheel. It is a Justice wheel. It is a wheel of love. It is a wheel of the Crucifixion. It is a wheel of Salvation. It is a wheel of Alpha and Omega. It is a wheel of light. It is a wheel of force. These wheels have centers of the cross. They are powered by the spirit and power of God the Creator.

The Universality of the Cross

The cross is old. It is older than human beings and civilization. God created the cross in the first chapter of the 1" verse of Genesis when he created the heaven and the earth in the beginning. The cross was created before religion. It predates humankind and human institutions. God created the cross when God created trillions of stars, solar systems, the earth and trillions of other celestial bodies in the galaxies. God created the cross when he created Crisscrosses of north and south, east and west.

The cross is at the heart of art, science, laws of nature and religion.

The trillions of radiant and brilliant sun rays that burst forth in every direction are replete with light rays of crosses emanating from the perpetual exploding light of the sun. The gravitational force of the earth as with other planetary bodies, creates crosses as it attracts objects of mass directly to its center of gravity in straight lines from the whole surface of the earth. This attracting gravitational force towards the center of the earth is so accurate that it makes possible straight perpendicular plumb lines with the surface of the earth. This gravitational force makes possible the achievement of a level surface. It not only causes one drop of water to fall straight to the earth, but it gives the curvature shape of the oceans around the earth and holds oceans, seas and rivers in their place on the surface of the earth. Since there is an opposite correlating gravitational force on the surface around the earth, these opposite forces of gravity form a cross. The geocentricity of the earth is a marvelous creation of God. In the book of Job written before the advent of science between four and six hundred years B.C., it says, "He stretched out the north over the empty place and hangeth the earth upon nothing." (Job 26:7 KJV).

The cross is so common and replete on earth, in the world and in our society that it is not possible to single the cross out as a religious or Christian symbol. The Cross is at the center of art and religion. It gives balance, congruence and connections to art, science, religion and law.

There is a cross at every intersection of streets. In the City of Atlanta, Martin Luther King, Jr. Drive runs from east to west and divides the City of Atlanta into northside and southside. Peachtree Street in the City of Atlanta runs from south to north and divides the City of Atlanta into the east side and the west side. The intersection of Peachtree Street and MLK Jr. Drive makes a geometric cross in the City of Atlanta. Also, Expressway 1-20 runs from east to west through the City of Atlanta and Expressways 1-75 and 1-85 intersects and divides the metro regions into north and south and east and west. Expressway 1-285 circles Atlanta and the metro region. Expressway I-285 becomes a wheel around the hub of the inner city of Atlanta. I-285 crosses I-20 on the east and west sides. I-285 crosses 1-75 and I-85 on the north and south sides. At every intersection, there is a cross.

Airplanes are crosses. They are modeled after flying birds and other fowl that fly. When a bird flies, it spreads its wings horizontally and extends its feet and legs horizontally when in flight. Railroad tracks use cross ties to support the metal rails and trains. There are benevolent and business organizations known as Red Cross and Blue Cross. There are crosswalks, crosswords, crossways, cross fingers, cross legs, cross eyes and many other words associated with the cross.

There is no way to restrict the cross or get the cross out of society. The cross is a universal phenomenon and a universal symbol that transcends religion, Law, art and science. God has created man as a creature that can lie horizontally, level to the ground. Man can stand erect in a vertical position. While standing in a vertical position, a man can stretch his arms straight out from the shoulder in opposite directions, parallel to the ground. (No other earthly creature can stand erect as a man.) With erect vertical posture and horizontally outstretched arms, man becomes a cross within himself. The cross is a part of man's structural design. The crucifix of Christ blends in with the cross.

The Vertical Dimension Message

There are obvious and explicit parallels and correlations between the creation of God in the universe and the revelation of God found in his Word in the book of the Bible and in the visitation of Jesus Christ who came in the flesh and dwelt among us (John 1:14 KJV). The universe and the Bible have a common source and a common purpose. The source is God. The same God who created the universe also inspired the revelatory writing of the Bible. The spirit behind God's creation is the same spirit that reveals itself in the Holy Scriptures of the Bible. The common purpose of God's creation in the universe and God's and God's revelation in the Bible is God's self-disclosure to humanity. God uses God's principles and laws of science, art, justice and religion to communicate God's truth, ways, will, love and mercy to mankind. The Bible is the greatest and most fascinating story ever told. It is the story of the secular and the sacred, the human and the divine. It is the meeting place of man and God at the horizontal and the vertical dimensions of the cross.

God is Not a Secret

God is not a secret. God is no longer far away. He has been made near by the blood of Christ (Ephesians 2:13, KJV). "The heavens declare the glory of God, and the firmament showeth his handywork (Psalm 19:1). God's creation is not a theory. It is a reality and more than a reality. God's creation and his glory are a supernatural divine reality. It is older than time and age. It is bigger than the size and dimensions. And yet, God's reality is definite, concrete, objective, quantifiable, visible and invisible. God provides the highest form of evidence and infallible proofs. God provides solids, such as solid rocks, hard iron, tough steel, dense lead and pure gold. God provides liquids over 70% of the earth's surface in rivers and oceans. God provides various kinds of vapors and gases. He provides the atmosphere with oxygen, which is essential for breathing and life.

The Marvels of the Earth

The earth is not a theory. It is one of the marvels of God's creation. It is the place of human habitation. It is the planetary place where God made himself known to mankind and where Jesus Christ visited and was lifted (Acts 1:9-11). According to The World Book Encyclopedia, the earth is at least 4½ billion years old. It is approximately 8 thousand miles in diameter. Its Equatorial circumference is 24,901.55 miles. It is like a big ball with over 70% of its surface covered with water. It has a spinning motion that rotates completely approximately every 24 hours, creating night and day. As it spins it also is traveling in its orbit around the sun. It completes its revolution around the sun every 365 days while traveling at a speed of 66,600 miles per hour. The earth makes this 595 million-mile journey each year. It is amazing that God created a spherical shaped ball of water in the sky that is perpetually spinning and revolving at incredible speeds and the inhabitants of the earth cannot detect the movement of the earth. The round water-surfaced earth spins around the round sun in the round orbit, around the sun with the geometrics of the round wheel and the nucleus of the cross.

God has created laws that govern the order of God's universe. God has created gravitational and magnetic laws. God created laws to govern light and sound. He created laws to govern the freezing points, melting and evaporation points of various substances. He creates laws of physics, chemistry, biology, mathematics and other natural sciences. He creates laws that govern the reproduction and the sustenance of plants and animals.

The creation reveals knowledge about its Creator. As we resort to the anthropomorphic descriptions of the nature of God, we can see descriptions of God through God's handywork. When we observe beautiful sunsets and sunrises with varying colors and formations of clouds, we can see the artist behind God's creation. When we observe the celestial majesty of the stars and moon in the sky by night and the clear blue sky by day with its floating clouds, we can see that God is an artist with aesthetic expressions of beauty. God is the creator of science, Art, Law and religion. There is balance (justice) and equilibrium in God's creation.

God's creation is infinitely beyond the most exaggerated imagination and understanding of mankind. However, God created man in such a marvelous way, that man is a witness to God's creation. In addition to, and congruent with God's creation, God created light and the eyes of man to see God's marvelous creation. Man has certain senses of seeing, hearing, smelling, feeling and intuiting. Man comes from the dust of the earth. He is sustained by the earth. Upon his demise, the man returns to the dust of the earth. Man can reason that the same God who created the heavens and the earth also created mankind. The book of Genesis confirms the common creator of the heavens and the earth along with man (Genesis 1:26-28).

God made man the kind of being who has self-awareness and can become an object to himself. God gives man an awareness of man's own existence and creaturehood in relation to the creator. Man has a nature that desires to relate to God. The soul and the spirit of man are more than the dust of the earth.

CHAPTER 3

GOD's CREATION AND BIBLICAL REVELATION

The Bible and God's universal creation provide compelling evidence that the God who created the universe is the same God who provides the revelation of his disclosure to man in the Bible and in Jesus Christ. The universe is a marvel of creation beyond the most exaggerated imagination. On the other hand, the Bible is an unfathomable and inexhaustible revelation of God's will and purpose for man.

Although the Bible was written (much of it) in the pre-scientific, pre-modern, and primeval times, it contains the only known authoritative unified and credible story as to how the world and life got started. The Bible is the oldest document containing a unified story with continuity about the beginning and the end and beyond history.

The Bible is also the only credible story about God, creation, revelation of God, God's relationship with man and his will for mankind on the earth. It is amazing that this oldest story was told and written at a time when man had less knowledge, less information and less knowledgeable resources and educational instruments.

That fact alone is a declaration that the truths and revelations of the Bible come from a source much higher and much more powerful than man. It seems that God chose a time in history before the advent of science, industrialization, or modernization to reveal to the world his revelation and salvation plan for man.

Science is the most recent outpost of religion. Religion developed through the process of God's revelations to man and man's response to those revelations. Man discovered the revelations of God through man's search for and discovery of God's revelations. So, religion is the oldest approach to life by man. Religion is man's efforts to understand and relate to God. Religion is the parent of all the other endeavors of man. Out of religion came belief systems, customs, social order, government, laws, art, education and industry. The aesthetics of art came out of religion as man sought to express beauty, harmony and some form of elevated thoughts of truth, ideas, joy, and happiness. Art is an elevated thought, spoken, written or otherwise represented.

Science is the most recent outpost of religion. The impact of science has been the most dramatic. Science has brought about more social, cultural and environmental changes in the past two hundred years than had taken place in the past five thousand years.

God chose to reveal himself in the Bible long before Columbus sailed to America in 1492 and before the Protestant Reformation of the 15 century; and before the English colonies began in 1607 and before the Declaration of

Independence of July 4, 1776. God chose to reveal himself before the Wright Brothers had their first successful airplane flight in Kitty Hawk, NC on December 17, 1903. God revealed himself in the Bible before the development of radio, telephone, television, atomic bomb, out of space travel, the computer and the internet. The world in the 21st century could not be more different than it was two thousand and six thousand years ago. At the same time, God's message given two thousand years ago and six thousand years ago could not be more relevant in this complex, perplexing and confusing 21st century.

Since true religion grew out of God's down reach for man and man's upreach to God, man must take the message of God seriously. Man's salvation and survival depend on heeding the message of God. This vertical relationship between man and God developed true religion. This true religion gave birth to divine laws, sacred art and secular science.

Since religion gave birth to divine laws, sacred art and secular science, these offsprings of religion are obligated to be loyal and obedient to the parenthood of the religion that gave them birth. They must remain loyal and obedient to the commandments and the authority of the God-inspired word of God contained in scripture.

True religion did not come out of man-made statutory laws or secular customs, science or traditions. True religion came from above. Therefore, the authority and validity of divine laws, art and science reside in religion under the authority of

God and Jesus Christ. The will of God is revealed clearly in Jesus Christ. God has firmly established his authority over his creation, mankind and the earth through the authoritative word of the Bible and by his only Begotten Son, Jesus Christ. No person, no race of people and no nation of people are exempt from the authority and jurisdiction of God. Romans states this authority and jurisdiction of God succinctly, "Let every soul be subject unto the higher powers. For there is no power but God: the powers that be are ordained of God." (Romans 13:1):

In this book of Ezekiel Saw the Wheel, the compelling, invincible and infallible evidence is presented to show through religion, law, art and science that the God who created the universe also revealed and revealed himself in his creation, the Bible and in Jesus Christ. This book connects the creation of God of the universe to the revelation of God in the Bible and in Jesus Christ. God is the author of divine laws, natural laws, art, religion and science. Therefore, it is impossible and ludicrous to attempt to exclude God from life or any part of his creation. Finite, mortal man is not qualified or capable of placing any limitations or conditions upon the omnipotent, omniscient, infinite, omnipresent eternal God. It is utter arrogance, deceptive, delusionary pride on the part of man to deny God's existence and God's connection with his creation and God's relationship with his creation and with his special relationship to humanity through Jesus Christ, the Savior.

Human beings and all the world are surrounded by the ever presence and reality of God. For in him we live, and move, and have our being (Acts 17:28). Despite this overwhelming evidence of the presence and reality of God, there are audacious persons in high and low secular places who are working feverishly to remove the name and any references to God, the Bible and Christ from the American culture in the 21" century. Sadly, many of these vain and futile efforts are finding their way into statutory law and government policies and procedures. The efforts to remove the name and influence of God from his creation are more difficult and futile than it would be to kick Stone Mountain of Georgia over the moon. However futile and vain these anti-Christ and anti-God efforts may be; they must be challenged and defeated by the historically documented and validated truth of religion, divine laws, natural laws, art and science. Anti-Christ and anti-God spirits are disobedient and rebellious spirits against truth, light, righteousness and life itself. Spirits in rebellion against God are dangerous and self-destructive. They must not be allowed to operate unchecked and unchallenged.

God Is Mindful of Man

There is solid evidence that God has a special love and favor toward man. According to Genesis, " so God created man in his own image, in the image of God created he him; male and female created he them." (Genesis 1:27). God also gave man dominion over every living thing (Genesis 1:28). The whole Bible is centered around God's agonizing concern for the salvation of man. Not only did God make man in his image in Genesis, but God became like man in Jesus Christ when he was born to Mary and Joseph. "And the Word was made flesh, and dwelt among us." (John 1:14). God has used his prophets, priests, angels, ministers and other messengers to communicate to and with man.

God has created in man the kind of creature who witnesses the creation of God and who develops interactive relationships with God's creation. God has given man the intelligence and the faculties of discernment to witness and understand the intelligible (knowable by man) universe. God has given man the vantage point on the earth to witness the earth, the oceans, the mountains, the moon, the sun and the stars. God has given man a front seat to witness the lighted, visible splendors of God's magnificent creation. God has given man a soul that savors the beauty of flowers, and the harmonious sound of music. soothing words, intriguing ideas, inspiring spirits, enlightening thoughts, transcending dreams and transforming visions. The Psalmist exclaims the goodness and the favor of God when he says, "Thou madest him to have dominion over the works of thy hands; thou hast put all things under his feet... O Lord, our Lord, how excellent is thy name in all the earth!" (Psalm 8:6, 9).

God has given man the intelligence and the reasoning to understand God's natural laws, divine laws, moral laws, scientific laws, justice, righteousness, beauty and goodness.

God creates reality and truth and gives man the discernment to make distinctions between right and wrong, good and evil, true and false, light and darkness, up and down, cold and hot, sweet and bitter, just and unjust, righteousness and unrighteousness, spiritual and carnal, divine and human, life and death. God has shown his favor for man.

Man's Spiritual Lag

God created man with a lofty nobility: "For thou hast made him a little lower than the angels, and has crowned him with glory and honour." (Psalms 8:5). Man is the crown of God's creation. God has given man thousands of years to obey him and live righteously according to the commandments of God. God's people have continued to disappoint God. How wonderful would the world be if man would live up to the potential that God has given him? The earth would be a paradise. If man would do God's will on earth as it is in heaven, it would truly be heaven on earth.

However, the disobedience of the secular man and the secular society is transforming the earth into a place of chaos, confusion and torment. God has given man thousands of years to improve his moral behavior and perfect his spirituality. As we look back five thousand years, man has made substantial progress in the physical environment. He has built ships, cities, tunnels, trains, motor vehicles, planes and a multitude of instruments and armaments. Man's inclination seems to have been to major in the physical environment and neglect his nature as a spiritual being. Man's external ambition was demonstrated when a man attempted to build the Tower of Babel (Genesis 11:1-9).

The great tragedy of man's life and his perilous predicament in the 21st century is his external physical ambitions and the gross neglect of his inner being and spiritual nature. The neglected, undeveloped, immature inner spiritual beings are not capable of, "replenishing the earth, subduing it, and having dominion over every living thing that moves upon the earth." (Genesis 1:27-28). God has given man over five thousand years to prepare himself mentally, morally, spiritually, socially and physically for the globalization that has been thrust upon the world in the 21st century. Man has had two thousand years since the coming of Christ to be ready to live in a global, culturally diverse world in peace.

God has given man thousands of years, God's word, truth, ways, wisdom, knowledge and his will in the Bible and in Christ. And yet, man is still spiritually lagging in darkness, ignorance and unrighteousness as the world spins toward the brink of disaster.

God Blessed America

Interestingly, God blessed America with sound founding doctrines from the Judeo-Christian Bible, beginning in the English colonies in the early 1600's A.D. Although this Judeo-Christian foundation was tarnished by the importation of Negro slaves in Jamestown, VA in 1619, God blessed

America. God blessed America with the Great Awakenings, beginning in 1726. There were large numbers of Christian revivals in the colonies. Christian preachers went throughout the colonies preaching evangelistic messages. Massive numbers of persons were converted. These 13 colonies spread Christianity throughout the United States before and subsequent to the signing of the Declaration of Independence on July 4, 1776.

What is interesting about God's blessing America is the fact that God gave America time to see her faults realize her mistakes and make amends. It took America 246 years (1619-1865, the Jamestown, VA enslavement to the Emancipation Proclamation). America also fought a civil war during this emancipation period. America's natural borders (especially the Atlantic and Pacific Oceans) protected the nation from foreign enemy invasions.

America, itself, was blessed with the invention of the airplane by the Wright Brothers of Kitty Hawk, NC on December 17, 1903. God continues to give America time to reconcile with its people and get its domestic house in order. A former slave by the name of Booker T. Washington, founded a school, Tuskegee Institute in Tuskegee, Alabama in 1881. The leadership of Booker T. Washington and the influence of the Tuskegee Institute generated significant influence throughout the segregated South and the nation. On September 18, 1895, Booker T. Washington gave his famous Cotton Exposition Speech in Atlanta, Georgia. It reverberated for good around the world ("Cast Down Your

Buckets Where You Are"). There were also many other positive race relations influences in America.

God continued to bless America, even with its racial segregation, discrimination and lynchings. As we look back in retrospect, we can see the missed opportunities to bring about racial justice and harmony for the nation. In 1941, the Japanese attacked Pearl Harbor and involved America in World War II. The South and much of America were still racially segregated. Through some high-powered maneuvering, the racially segregated air base in Tuskegee, Alabama was permitted to use its exceptional aviation skills in Europe in World War II. The United States developed and used the Atomic Bomb on Hiroshima and Nagasaki in 1945 to bring a close to World War II.

The moral and spiritual lag in America could not be more dramatically illustrated than when the Black American soldiers returned to America after the war ended in 1945, they returned to a racially segregated society. Thousands of Black American soldiers died in the war. Those Black soldiers who returned; returned to the low social status of second-class citizenship in America, especially in the South.

God blessed America. America came out of the war victoriously. This young country, one hundred sixty-nine years after its Declaration of Independence, saved Europe in World War II. President Dwight D. Eisenhower said some insightful words about America. "America is great because she is good. If she ceases to be good, she will cease to be great." Has America ceased to be good? Is this spiritual moral lag dragging America down from its greatness? Are the curses of America diminishing and eclipsing the blessings?

It took approximately twenty years after the end of World War II from 1945 to 1965 to get Civil Rights Laws on the Books to protect the Civil Rights of the Black Americans. It also required extraordinary efforts and sacrifice on the part of the Black Americans to influence the Nation to pass laws to protect their human rights and person. Why did the spiritual lag make it necessary for Dr. Martin Luther King, Jr. and others to have to sacrifice their lives for human rights which appeared to be so obvious and self-evident?

Late-But Great Lesson

God has given humanity over 5,000 years to obey God's commandments and get humanity's house In order. Man's 5,000-year history is replete with rebellion against God and disobedience to righteousness and justice. The consequences have been wars. rumors of wars, pain and suffering. God is patient, merciful and forgiving. However, there are dire consequences to the violations of God's laws. God has always given man a clear and invincible warning about the consequences of disobedience. God warned Adam and Eve about the consequences of the forbidden tree (Genesis 2:16-17). However, this spiritual lag in the 21st century in America takes on a most unique and serious connotation.

God began his conversation with man from a global and universal perspective in the book of Genesis. God talked about the earth as we have alluded to earlier. However, the early primeval and ancient historical people were preoccupied with their local village and local community life. These local villages and primitive environments prevailed for thousands of years. The full impact of globalization has been with America and most of the world for less than 100 years.

The vast social changes in the past 100 years have been profound and overwhelming due primarily to the advancement in scientific technology. Somehow, these vast social changes are accompanied by a decay in moral and spiritual values. At a time when more social cohesion is needed to counteract the onslaught of cultural diversity, there are more divisive ideologies, and moral, political and cultural corruption. The acceleration of these strange heterogeneous social forces has placed America in a most precarious predicament.

In order for us to understand more clearly our human predicament and cultural crisis as Americans in this 21st century, we must understand that injustice creates deficits in human potential. We must understand that justice is a requirement of God. The denial and the delay of justice compound the damages, the deficits and the costs to the victims, as well as to the nation.

The subject of social injustice in America during the four-hundred-year history is spoken of in a broad sense. The social injustice in America is not restricted to the U.S. Government.

It includes corporate, business and individual injustices as well. The combined injustices during this four-hundred-year history of America have created great deficits and serious damage to countless victims and the nation itself. As a result of these deficits, America is faced with a very serious problem.

There have been too many forfeitures of justice; too many missed opportunities; too many accumulated wrongs; too many old unpaid debts; and too many accumulated liabilities over too long a period of time. There has been too much arrogance and selfish pride. There has been too much irresponsibility and abuse of freedom and authority. There is too much mundane irreverence to God. There are too many violations of the U.S. Constitution and the Divine Laws of God.

The New American Dilemma

How can a divided, fractured and vulnerable America safeguard itself from external and internal enemies and pay the compounded debts that it owes to so many for so long? There are a number of things that make America more vulnerable to sabotage and violent attacks than ever before. America has a cherished tradition of individual liberty, civil rights and freedom. America also has a liberal indiscriminate open invitation to the world. America is very tolerant and accommodating to foreign ideologies and traditions. America is also becoming less tolerant of some of its own ideologies and traditions, especially in regard to Christianity.

America is a country that is tilting more towards secularism than ever before in its history. America is accommodating more cultural diversity, religious pluralism, heterogeneity and internationalism than any other country on the globe. How does a nation keep its own national identity in the midst of a growing internal internationalism?

Globalization through electronic technology is the other significant factor that is exacerbating the new American dilemma. The advancement in aviational technology, the computer, internet, smart cell phones, GAP (Global Positioning System), RFID (Radio Frequency Identification), FAX machines and the growing social media has created a network of globalization on the earth. Unfortunately, America never leads responsibly in preparing its citizens and its people for major and massive social change. There was no adequate preparation for the Emancipation Proclamation in 1865. There was no adequate preparation for the integration of public schools in 1954. There was no adequate preparation for the integration of public accommodations in the passage of the 1964 Civil Rights Act. There has not been adequate preparation for the accommodation of 50 million immigrants to the United States in the past fifty years. There has not been adequate preparation to accommodate all American citizens with on line entitled services. There has been a lack of leadership in preparing the American people for cultural diversity and religious pluralism in the democratic society of

America. The American culture crisis is now heading for the American National identity crisis.

The new American dilemma arises out of long years of negligence, debts and deficits, the influx of diverse maladaptive social ethnicities, advanced electronic and nuclear technology and a network of globalization. This means that communications, disseminations and transmissions that in the past required months and years to accomplish, can now be accomplished in seconds, minutes and hours. Things that used to require physical and visible transport can now be conveyed through inaudible and invisible electronic signals. This highlights the vulnerability, invasion of privacy and accessibility to all persons and nations on the earth.

The new American dilemma is simply this, that more demands can now be placed on the Nation within a short period of time than is possible for the Nation to provide adequate response. Requests and demands can be made so very quickly now. In order to be able to respond sufficiently, the Nation needs surpluses and not debtors and deficits.

This invasion of privacy, vulnerability and accessibility has brought home a significant truism. It makes sense to be your brother's keeper. It makes sense to love God, love your neighbor and love your enemies. At the end of the day, anything less than love, will not be sufficient for our salvation and survival on the planet Earth. More and more our earthly fate is in the hands of strangers.

Why did God allow a man to languish in the crudeness of primitive societies using homemade and crude tools for over 5,000 years? God wanted to give man time to appreciate life and to live in harmony, peace, goodwill and brotherhood. Sadly, that after 5.000 years and 2,000 years after the coming of Christ, man has not reached an acceptable level of humane civilization and socialization. We cannot say that God did not give man enough time. We cannot say that God deprived man of the glory of his creation. The earth, the moon, the sun and the stars have always been a part of man's natural environment. We cannot say that God did not speak to man's mind and his spirit. The Biblical record is there. We cannot say that God did not make it plain. God sent his only Begotten Son to this earth to live and reveal the loving heart of God through the crucifixion, resurrection and ascension back to God.

God blessed America. God has been patient with America. God has given America 400 years of blessings. America has had enough time to transform the neighborhood into a brotherhood. God has blessed America to be the leading nation of the world. However, not only is America retreating from this noble position, a substantial number of Americans are becoming anti to the God who has bountifully blessed the Nation of America.

How wonderful it would be if we lived in a world where all people were members of the household of God. Over five thousand years and two thousand years after the coming of Christ, we are still living among strangers. However, the ideal is still there as expressed so beautifully by Paul, "Now therefore ye are no more strangers and foreigners, but fellow citizens with the saints, and of the household of God." (Ephesians 1:19).

Technology and Morality

The power and the instruments of technology have exceeded man's morality and spirituality to guide and control. This emphasis on secularism (the removal of Godly influences from the culture) has created a serious spiritual vacuum in American society. Since nature "abhors a vacuum," this vacated spiritual capacity is being filled with alien and demonic spirits. The alien demonic spirits of evil and darkness are looking for empty vacated spiritual capacities. The mixture of alien and demonic spirits with modern technology makes a most lethal combination. Children and all human beings have spiritual capacities. All human agencies and institutions have spiritual capacities. The secular society of America is encouraging to leave vacant the human spiritual capacities created by God.

The Spirit of God is seeking to fill these spiritual and moral capacities of human beings who are made in the image (Genesis 1:27) of God. The Spirit of God and the Spirit of the love of God are the only safe and worthy spirits to dwell in the hearts of humans. The Bible teaches explicitly to test the spirits to see whether they are of God (1 John 4:1-3). To the extent that the anti-God and the antichrist spirits prevail in

America (and other places as well), to the same extent, the blind demonic use of technology will destroy human life and the values of civilization.

The spiritual morality of God and the secular use of technology are in serious competition. Technology is not evil within itself. Technology can be used for good or evil. Since one evil technological act can cause massive devastation and destruction; can we, God's children, afford to neglect the spiritual capacities, that will determine how technology will be used?

It should be obvious to honest and serious observers, that technology is already beyond the responsible control of man. God made the salvation knowledge available thousands of years before the birth of science and technology. The disobedient ways of man have failed to place him in a position to save himself from the devices of his own hands. Now is a must time to listen to the message that God has been giving him for thousands of years. We must stay reminded that the resistance of man to the salvation message of God is so strong that Jesus who came with a heart full of love and healing power was crucified.

What has changed in two thousand years that could possibly cause a man to look at Christ differently today than he did two thousand years ago? Man's lie of independence that he can get along without God has failed. Man has exhausted all of his ungodly remedies and his problems are getting progressively worse. These wheels of seasons, wheels of time, wheels of numbers, wheels of direction and wheels of

Justice are moving to the cataclysmic end time where options are narrowed to accept Jesus Christ or perish.

CHAPTER 4

THE POWER OF TWO LINES

First, let us consider the minus (-) sign in mathematics. The minus sign is a negative sign. It subtracts. It takes from the total of another value. The minus suggests a deficit. It minimizes the quantity or quality of another value. It suggests a loss. The minus sign is also used as a dash of a hyphen between two words. In both instances, the minus sign stands alone. The minus sign is basic in mathematical operations.

The minus sign is a horizontal line. Regardless of how long the horizontal line is, it is still a deficit symbol. This horizontal line is used as a dash on tombstones between the dead person's birth date and deceased date. The minus sign suggests limitations and reduction. The minus sign has a larger symbolic meaning. It is symbolic of the secular dimension. The secular dimension is the worldly dimension. It is the dimension of humanism. Humanism is defined by what man can do without any appeal or help from a higher authority.

The horizontal secular dimension reveals a profound truth about the horizontal dimension. The truth is that man cannot realize lasting salvation on the horizontal level. Man has a need for another and higher dimension. The needed dimension, of course, is the vertical dimension.

When the vertical line is added to the horizontal line, the symbol becomes a plus sign. The plus sign is the positive sign. It is a sign of addition. The vertical line has transformed the horizontal line into a plus sign. The plus sign has now become a positive sign which adds, instead of subtracting. This gives an indication of the power of the two lines. The crossing or the connection of these two lines has brought about a new function and a new power. It is the power of addition which totals a sum of the individual collective numbers. One plus any other number or collection of numbers can become one sum or one total inclusive number. The plus sign shows how many can be one and one can be many.

Multiplication (x)

The multiplication (x) sign is another form of the cross. This form of the cross involves the connection or the crossing of two diagonal lines. The standard cross consists of a horizontal line intersected by a vertical line (+). However, the intersecting of the diagonal lines indicates the power of the intersection and the crossing of two lines. There is power in the touching (the intersection) of the diagonal-lined cross. It has the power of multiplying. The multiplication sign is called the time sign (x). The power of multiplication increases significantly the product of the numbers involved. For example, 5+5=10. However, 5x5=25. We are still demonstrating the power of the cross (two intersecting lines). The positive plus (+) has the potential to increase added quantities. The multiplication time sign (x) has the potential to increase multiplied quantities even more so over the addition of quantities.

It is significant to note that through human reproduction, special sex chromosomes determine whether the zygote will develop into a boy or a girl. Each body cell contains a pair of sex chromosomes. In females, the two sex chromosomes are identical. Each of the chromosomes is called an X chromosome. The cells of males have one X chromosome, and a smaller chromosome called the Y chromosome. At fertilization, a sperm with an X chromosome uniting with an egg will develop into a girl baby because the fertilized egg will have two X chromosomes. A sperm with a Y chromosome uniting with an egg will form a boy baby because the fertilized egg will have the X and Y combination. (World Book Encyclopedia, vol. Q.R. 16). It is important to paint out this most significant reproduction (multiplication) process involving the universal cross symbols of X and Y. It must be noted that the two X chromosomes of the woman are not sufficient for reproduction (multiplication). Neither are the X and Y chromosomes of the man sufficient for reproduction. It is significant that these X and Y chromosomes have connections and crosses with each other in order for multiplication to take place. The Y chromosome possessed by the male gives the appearance of being an incomplete X.

Although the Y is not an X, it has a long line and a short line. They both connect.

The Mathematical Division Symbol (÷)

The division symbol is very much unlike the plus sign (or symbol) (+) and the time sign (x). The significant difference between the division (÷) sign and the plus (+) and the time (x) sign is that the division sign is not a cross. However, the division sign constitutes a horizontal minus sign bordered between a period on top of the minus sign and a period beneath the minus sign. Notice that the two periods and the minus sign do not touch or connect with each other. They are three disconnected entities. They are distinctly separated from each other. Where there is no touching or connection there can be no addition or multiplication.

The division sign (÷) denotes two mathematical operations. They are subtraction and division. The negative minus sign stands for subtraction. The two periods disallow extensions and connections. Therefore, the division sign indicates a recessive, degenerative and diminishing process. The division is locked into the negative horizontal dimension.

When the division symbol is translated into the social and spiritual arena, it translates into human separation, alienation and degeneration. It minimizes and eliminates the possibility of human connections, touching and regeneration. The division sign is not a cross. It is the cross that connects with the horizontal and provides the vertical preach of hope and escape from the horizontal prison house of secularism. The cross makes possible reproduction, redemption and salvation through Jesus Christ. The cross has the power of translating a negative into a positive. The cross has the power of translating a minus sign into a plus sign.

The Power of the Cross

In order to glimpse the essence, significance and power of the cross, the Biblical perspective sheds insight. Consider the statement Paul makes to the Corinthians:

> For Christ sent me not to baptize, but to preach the gospel: not with wisdom of words, less the cross of Christ should be made of non-effect. For the preaching of the cross is to them that perish foolishness, but unto us which are saved it is the power of God (1 Cor. 1:17-18)

In other scriptures, Paul states that the foolishness of God is wiser than men, and the weakness of God is stronger than men (1 Corinthians 1:25). God does simple things that confound the wisdom of the world. The use of two lines of the horizontal and vertical dimensions of the cross is an example of simplicity that confounds the wise of this world.

Man is capable of assuming both dimensions of the cross. When a man lies resting and fully reclined, he is in a horizontal position. This resting position represents inactivity. The fragile human body needs periodic rest, sleep and inactivity for refreshing and restoration. The final demise is the horizontal position. The only hope for the final demise is the faith in the resurrected Jesus Christ.

Everyone is destined to end in the horizontal position level to the ground in the final resting place. The final horizontal position reinforces the meaning of the minus sign, the negative deficit subtracting sign.

When God created man in the image of God, he gave man a sign of hope by creating man to stand erect. Man is designed as a vertical erect creature. The other animals are designed as horizontal creatures. Most of them walk and move about on four legs. Most animals that live in water as their habitat, do not have legs. The bodies of fish are designed to be horizontal to the earth. The two-legged fowls that walk on the earth and fly, have horizontally designed bodies and or legs that are not vertical.

The vertical posture of man is a sign of hope and future possibilities. Man's body is designed like a cross with vertical and horizontal dimensions. Man is blessed to be able to wake up from horizontal slumber, get up, stand up, step up and look up. This creature, man, made in the image of God ought to be grateful as expressed by David: "I will praise thee; for I am fearfully and wonderfully made marvelous are thy works; and that my soul knoweth right well'" (Psalm 139:14).

Job wrestles with the nature and future of man's being in Job, chapter fourteen. He raises the baffling question, "If a man dies, shall he live again? All the days of my appointed time will I wait, till my change come." (Job 14:14). Jesus and the New Testament answer the question of Job. The sacrifice on the Cross and the resurrection and the ascension of Jesus provide the answer for eternal life.

Which Way is Up?

Up is the opposite of down for all who inhabit the planet Earth. Down points to the earth and below the earth to its center. Since the earth is spherical (round-shaped), persons on the opposite side of the earth are pointing in opposite directions when they point upward. So, technically speaking, up is the opposite of the force of gravity. Without a force strong enough to counter the force of gravity, all objects of mass are bound to the earth (or other respective planetary bodies).

God designed man's (human) body to stand vertically erect. Man's erect body is in alignment with the plumb line (Amos7:7-8) that the prophet Amos speaks about. Man is designed with a straight posture that minimizes the earth-bound effects of gravity and gives spiritual hope of overcoming this prison house of being earth-bound. The vertical design of man's body provides spiritual hope of rising to meet God. The American Negro slaves expressed this hope in many of their Negro Spirituals. Three spirituals come to mind: "Some Glad Morning When this Life is Over, I'll Fly Away," "Swing Low Sweet Chariot and Let Me Ride," and "I am Going Home to be with God."

The Bible teaches that "flesh and blood," cannot inherit the Kingdom of God (1 Corinthians 15:50). However, as we consider the power of the two lines of the cross, we can see the favor of God towards man. Jesus endured the cross to make it possible for man to have eternal life. Jesus confirms this hope and the power of the cross by his resurrection recorded in the Four Gospels and his ascension (Acts 1:9-11). The Bible, in the book of Acts, states he (Jesus) was, "taken up; and a cloud received him out of their sight." This ascension of Jesus concluded his promise in John 12:32, "And I, if I am lifted from the earth, will draw all men unto me."

CHAPTER 5

WHEELS OF CREATION AND REVELATION

THE WHEEL OF MATTER
CAN YOU SEE THE CROSS?
CREATIONISM

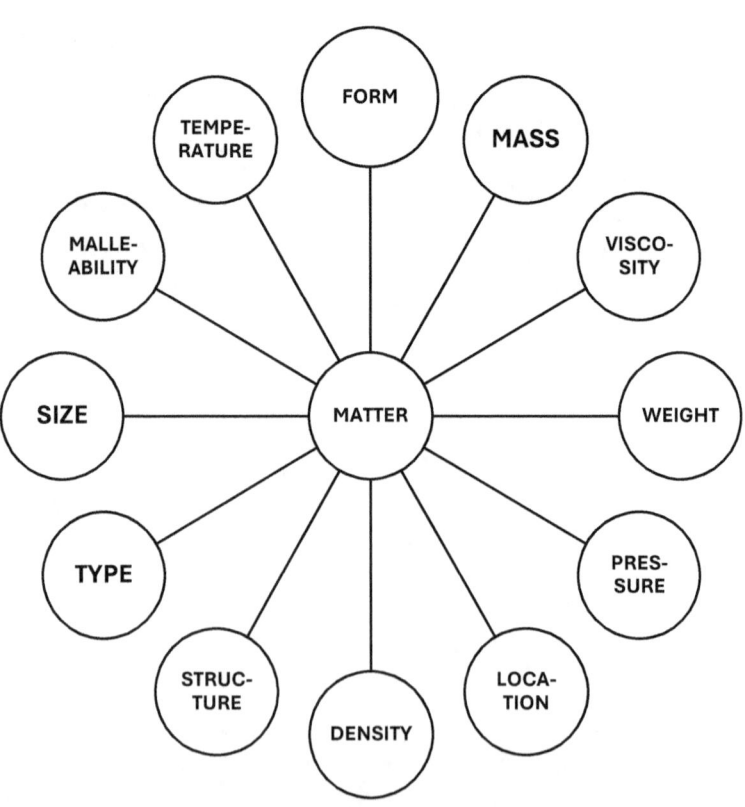

IN THE BEGINNING GOD CREATED THE HEAVEN AND THE EARTH (Genesis 1:1). God created matter in the beginning. We do not know when. Genesis declares that God did it and those of us who are blessed with eyes to see, we behold God's creation! Charles Darwin's Theory of Evolution is taught in schools. It is a theory (no facts to support or confirm) and it is acknowledged as such. However, the CREATIONISM OF GOD is of the highest factual evidence. And yet, most American schools prohibit or ignore the teaching of CREATIONISM in the Bible. The evidence of CREATIONISM is clear and convincing, infallible, undeniable, and infinitely overwhelming. The evidence is not hidden or obscured. GOD created matter (evidence) in three forms: (1) SOLIDS, (2) LIQUIDS, and (3) GASEOUS STATES. God went further and created human beings (consisting themselves of the three forms of matter) with EYES to see and EARS to hear the evidence; with HANDS to touch the evidence and with MINDS to analyze and synthesize the evidence of CREATIONISM. The heavens and earth on and all creatures below and existence, itself, declares the GLORY OF THE CREATOR, GOD!

THE WHEEL OF SEASONS
CAN YOU SEE THE CROSS?

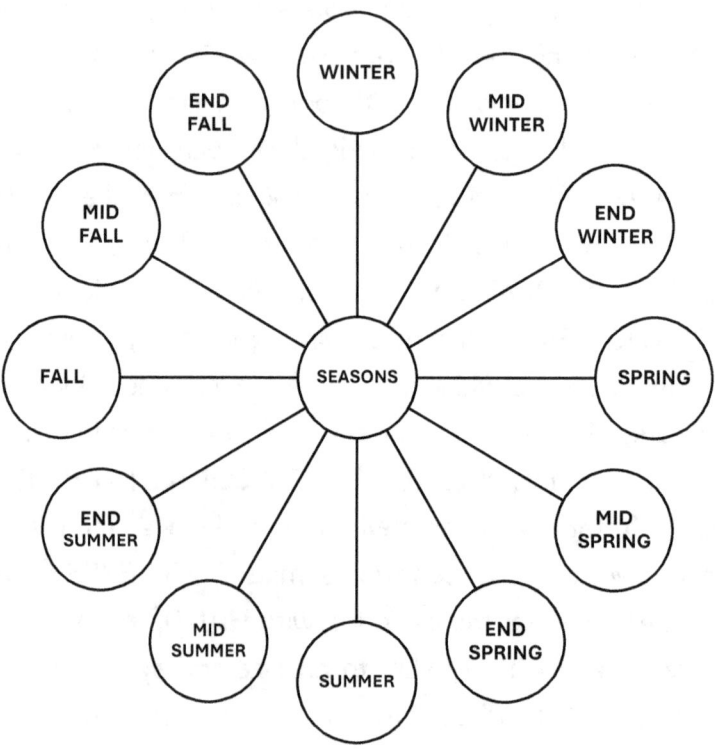

Where do seasons come from? That is a scientific question. However, before science arose, Genesis answered the question over four thousand years B.C. "And God said, Let there be lights in the firmament of the heaven to divide the day from the night; and let them be for signs, and for seasons, and for days, and years, And let them be for lights in the firmament of the heaven to give light upon the earth: and it was so (Genesis 1:14-15). The Bible is replete with references to seasons. Its accuracy is astounding considering the primitive and primeval societies that were in existence during the early times in which the Bible was written, and especially, Genesis. The truth of the Bible is confirmed by science. Science confirms that the earth spins on its axis at the rate of over a thousand miles per hour and completes the spinning rotation every 24 hours, giving us day and night. Science confirms that the earth revolves around the sun at the rate of 66,600 miles per hour (World Book Encyclopedia) and it travels 595,000,000 miles every three hundred sixty-five days. As the earth makes its journey around the sun, there are four distinct seasons. Creation and revelation are related.

THE WHEEL OF DIRECTION
CAN YOU SEE THE CROSS?

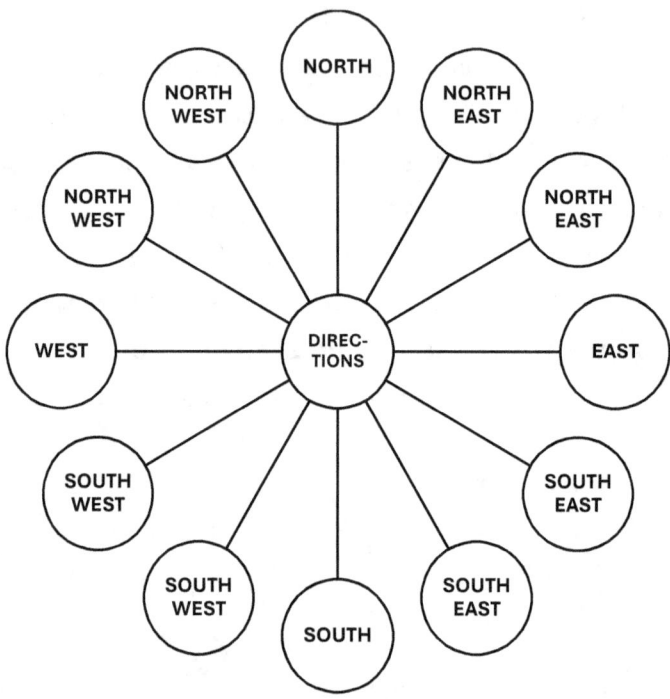

The creation presents a Creator who shows his favor towards mankind. God's creation is not arbitrary, chaotic or confusing. It is orderly and understandable to mankind. The creation has been fixed. reliable and predictable laws. He gave man the intelligence to learn about the laws of physics, chemistry, mathematics, and geometry astronomy, physiology, biology, anthropology, psychology. sociology, social science, electronics, radiology, medicine and the rest. Thousands of years before man developed scientific knowledge. God provided means by which man could navigate and negotiate his environment to nurture and safeguard life. Before the development of science, Job says the most amazing thing: "He stretcheth out the north over the empty place, and hangeth the earth on nothing." (Job 26:7). God created an environment so that man can find his way. God does not want man to be lost. God has given clear directions in his creation on the earth. The same God has given clear directions in the Holy Bible. The God of the creation of the universe is the same God of the revelation of the Bible.

THE WHEEL OF 12 MONTHS
CAN YOU SEE THE CROSS?

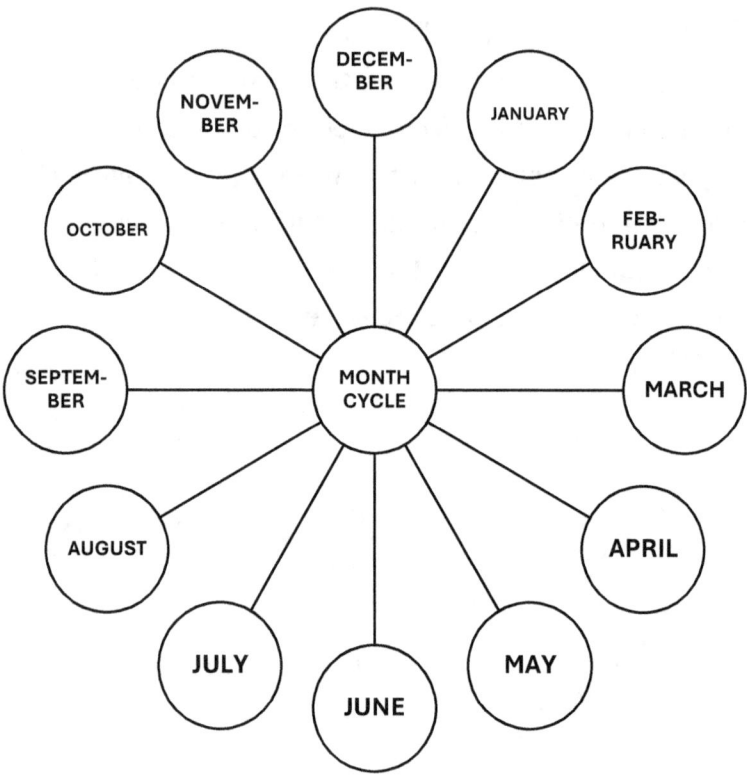

The twelve-month yearly cycle coincides with the four seasons of the year. The word, month, is referred to in the Bible 234 times (230 times in the Old Testament and 4 times in the New Testament.) Luke refers to month twice and Revelations refers to month twice. Again, it is interesting that Ezekiel has the highest number of references to the month, along with the book of Numbers. Each book, Ezekiel and Numbers, refers to MONTH 31 times. It is also interesting that Ezekiel and Numbers, refer to the plurality (MONTHS) the same number of times, being three. The total plurality (MONTHS) is used 59 times in the Bible. The plural (months) is used 16 times in the New Testament. It is not reasonable to believe that man in a primitive society, could have developed these complex cyclical occurrences. Easily, more commentary has been written on the Bible than any other book. However, the Bible, like the universe, is light years from being fully explored.

THE NUMBER LINE WHEEL
CAN YOU SEE THE CROSS?

+10
+9
+8
+7
+6
+5
+4
+3
+2
+1

10-9-8-7-6-5-4-3-2-1-0+1+2+3+4+5+6+7+8+9+10

-1
-2
-3
-4
-5
-6
-7
-8
-9
-10

It is obvious that these ten numbers are universal. They correspond to the ten fingers and the ten toes of human beings. These ten numbers are the universal foundation of mathematics. These ten numbers and zeros can be used to add, subtract, divide and multiply. They can be used in the most complex formulas, calculations and mathematical computations and operations. They correspond to the ten fingers and the ten toes of human beings. There is a relationship between these ten numbers and the human beings who use them to calculate and compute information. These ten numbers relate to math, science, law, art and religion. They relate to the truth of the cross. They have the horizontal dimension and they have the vertical dimension. The circumference of this cross makes a circle. The circle is a big Zero, Wheel or Sphere.

THE COMPASS LOCATION WHEEL
CAN YOU SEE THE CROSS?

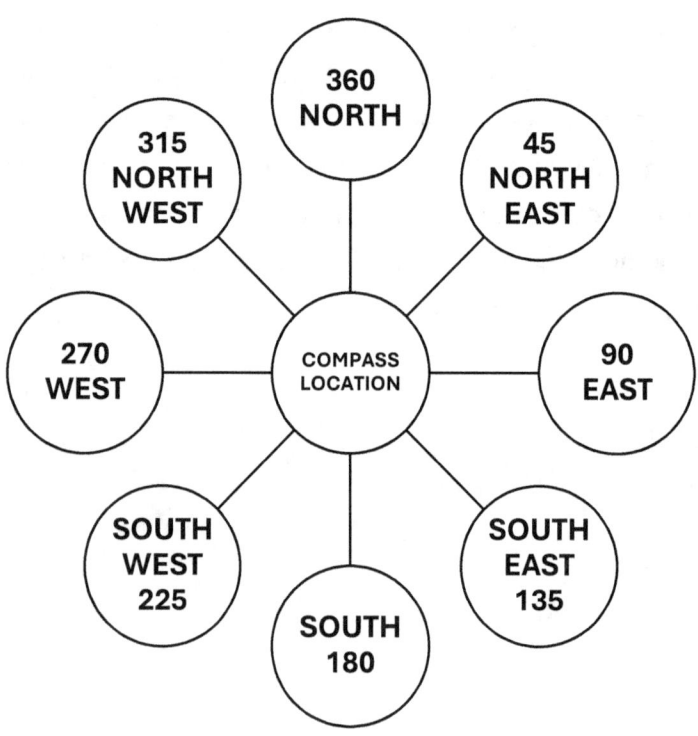

God has shown special favor to man (male and female) as to no other creature. "So, God created man in his own image, in the image of God created he him; male and female created he them." (Genesis 1:27). Additionally, God blessed them, and God said unto them, "Be fruitful, and multiply, and replenish the earth, and subdue it; and have dominion over the fish of the sea, and over the fowl of the air, and over every living thing that moveth upon the earth." (Genesis 1:28). God has given man scientific, artistic, lawful and spiritual knowledge to carry out the high and noble commandments to be "fruitful," "multiply," "replenish... and subdue the earth." and have, "dominion," over all creatures of the earth. God has given man the ability to discover and utilize the gravitational, magnetic and other resources, laws and forces of nature to carry God's commandments. Man uses the knowledge of math and science to make instruments to locate any space and place on the earth. In addition to the compass, man now uses a vocal GPS (global positioning system) for pinpointing directions and locations. The Creator of the universe is the Revelator of the Bible.

THE LEVEL AND THE PLUMB LINE
CAN YOU SEE THE CROSS?

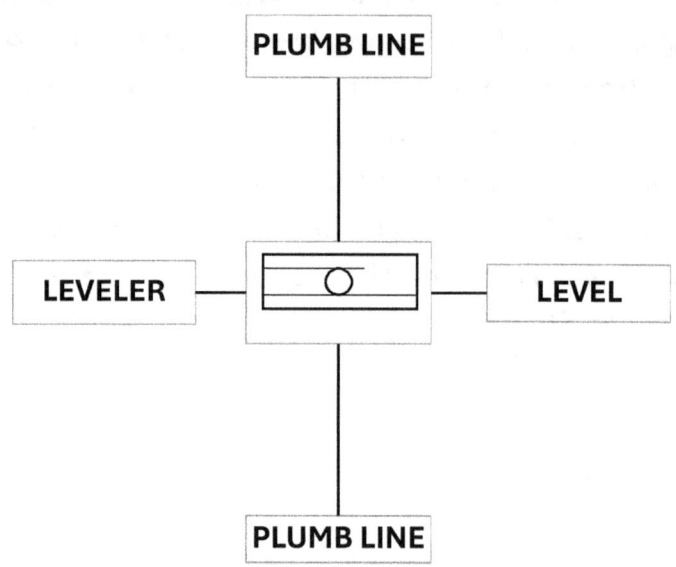

God made it possible through the law of gravity for man to achieve a level plane, horizontally and vertically, through the use of the level and the plumb line. The level is an instrument that carpenters and other building construction workers use to achieve a level surface. The level consists of a bar with a tube filled with a liquid that makes room for an air bubble. The centering of the bubble indicates the plane is level. It is the gravitational force that makes this bubble-measuring movement possible. The plumb line is the instrument that is used in construction to achieve a straight vertical line. The plumb line consists of a string or line with a weight at the bottom that causes it by the force of gravity to hang straight down all around. The plumb line is used as a vertical guide to ensure vertical straightness. As you can discern by the illustration above, there is a precise straight horizontal line and a precise vertical line that intersects with each other at the zero or bubble midpoint. The illustration is a cross. Amos advocated justice (Amos 5:24). God also told Amos (Amos 7:7-8) that. *I will set a plumb line in the midst of my people Israel." "I came down from Heaven." (John 6:38)

THE 12 HOUR CLOCK WHEEL
CAN YOU SEE THE CROSS?

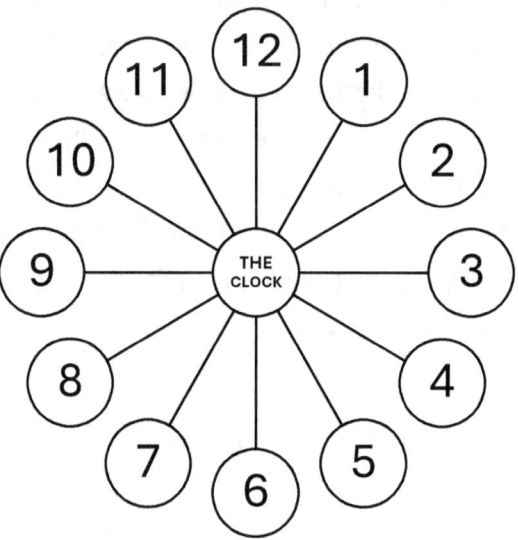

The time segment known as HOUR is referred to a total of 91 times in the Old Testament and the New Testament of the Bible (James Strong, LL.D., S.T.D.). However, HOUR is used only 4 times in the Old Testament. All 4 references are in the book of Daniels. Matthew uses HOUR 21 times, Mark uses it 9 times, Luke uses it 13 times, John uses it 21 times, Acts 9 times, I" Corinthians 3 times and Revelations uses HOUR 10 times. The plural (HOURS) is used only 3 times. Acts use it twice. John uses it once when Jesus answered, "Are there not twelve hours in the day?" (John 119). Again, the significance of the number twelve is highlighted in the Bible when it is used in correlation to the twelve hours of the day and twelve hours of the night which totals the 24 hours it takes for the earth spinning to make a complete revolution. The twenty-four-hour night and day cycle is compatible with the sleeping and awakening pattern of human beings. There is a synchronization between the activities and resources of the earth and the activities and needs of mankind on the earth. God is the Synchronizer.

THE WHEEL OF JUSTICE
CAN YOU SEE THE CROSS?

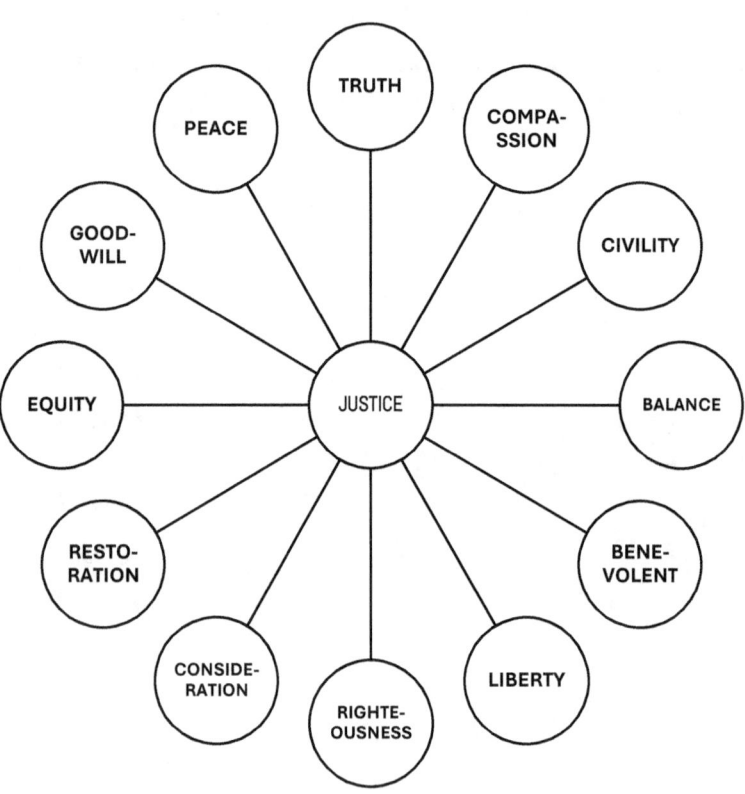

Justice represents the law. It is essential for balance and stability. Justice is that equitable force in human transactions that maintain an even balance in the exchange and distribution of values (Psychotrauma, W.J. Webb, page 95).

The phenomenon of justice, as it relates to balance, is interwoven with the natural environment. It involves symmetrical forms, blending patterns, mutual, reciprocal and complementary relationships. The universe is a cosmos, not chaos. The symbol for justice is the balanced scales with equal weight on each side. The prophet Amos prognosticated that justice ought to be free: "But let judgment run down as waters, and righteousness as a mighty stream." (Amos 5:24). The ways of justice are divine and eternal. Humanity and civilization could be advanced and enhanced significantly if the political, judicial and economic power structures would allow and encourage the turning of the, "wheels of justice." The benefits of justice are in, "the turning wheels of justice."

SCALES OF JUSTICE WHEEL
CAN YOU SEE THE CROSS?

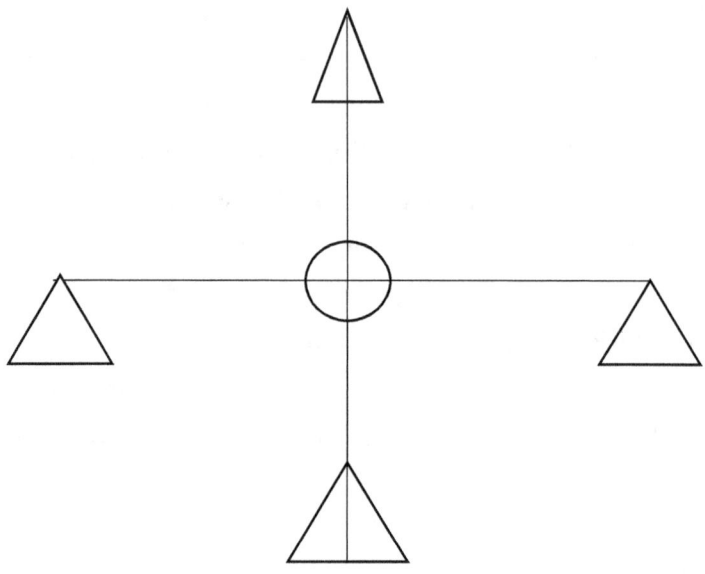

The Scales of Justice is a universal symbol. It shows measurement, balance and administration of justice. If the government respected and majored seriously in the administration of justice, human societies would be more peaceful, progressive and healthy. Justice is a concept of moral rightness based on ethics, rationality, law, religion, equity and fairness , as well as the administration of the law. Justice takes into consideration the inalienable and inherent rights of all human beings and citizens, the right of all people and individuals to the equal protection before the law of their civil rights without discrimination on the basis of race. disability, gender, color, ethnicity, religion, age, economic status and other characteristics regarded as being inclusive of social justice under the overall jurisdiction of the Divine Laws of God is the goal of justice. Injustice is an act of violence (Psychotrauma, W.J. Webb, p. 99). Injustice creates a deficit in the human potential. It leads to injuries, chaos, confusion and destruction. "My son, forget not my law; but let thine heart keep my commandments, for length of days and long life, and peace, shall they add to thee." (Proverbs 3:1-2)

WHEEL OF ISRAEL'S 12 TRIBES
CAN YOU SEE THE CROSS?

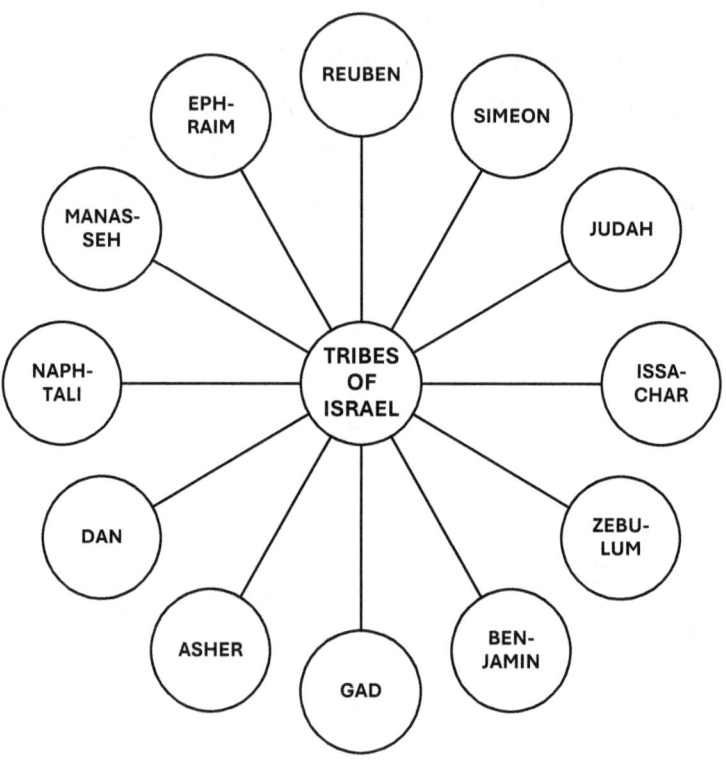

Jacob was the son of Isaac and Rebekah and the grandson of Abraham and Sarah. Jacob had twelve sons. The twelve tribes of Israel took the names of the twelve sons of Jacob. Jacob had six sons by his wife Leah and one daughter (Reuben, Simeon, Levi, Judah, Issachar, Zebulun, Dinah, Joseph and Benjamin). Jacob had two sons by Rachel's maid, Bilhah (Dan and Naphtali). Jacob had two sons by Leah's maid, Zilpah (Gad and Asher). Jacob dreamed of a ladder that reached from the earth to heaven (Genesis 28:12) with angels of God ascending and descending. Jacob's name was changed from Jacob to Israel by an unnamed man whom he wrestled with for a blessing (Gen. 32:24-32). The twelve Sons of Jacob somehow coincide with the significant number of wholeness of the number twelve. There are 186 references to the number twelve in the Bible. The biblical story that is unfolding is inextricably connected with the principles and powers of the universal God. Twelve completes significant time eyeless. Its significance is connected with the universe. It is connected with a power higher than mankind. There is a cross in every circle. In every cross, a circle can be made. The genealogy of Jesus is traced through Abraham, Isaac, Jacob and David. Jesus chose 12 disciples.

THE WHEEL OF CHRIST'S 12 DISCIPLES
CAN YOU SEE THE CROSS?

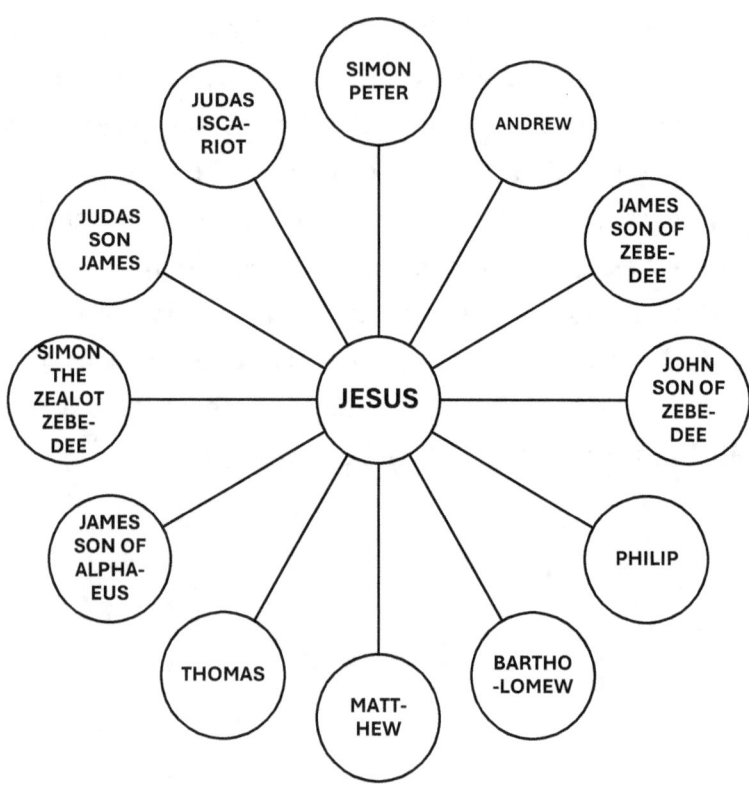

Somehow, it was significant for Jesus to choose twelve disciples. It is obvious that twelve was not an arbitrary number. Twelve makes a complete circle of three hundred sixty degrees. It is the number of twelve clock hours in the day. It is the number of months in the year. It corresponds with the cycle of the four seasons—winter, spring, summer and fall. It corresponds with the four directions— north, east, south and west. According to (James Strong, LL.D, S.T.D), the Bible has one hundred eighty-six (186) references to the number twelve. The twelve disciples correspond to the twelve tribes of Israel.

CHRIST'S CRUCIFIXION TIME CYCLE
CAN YOU SEE THE CROSS?

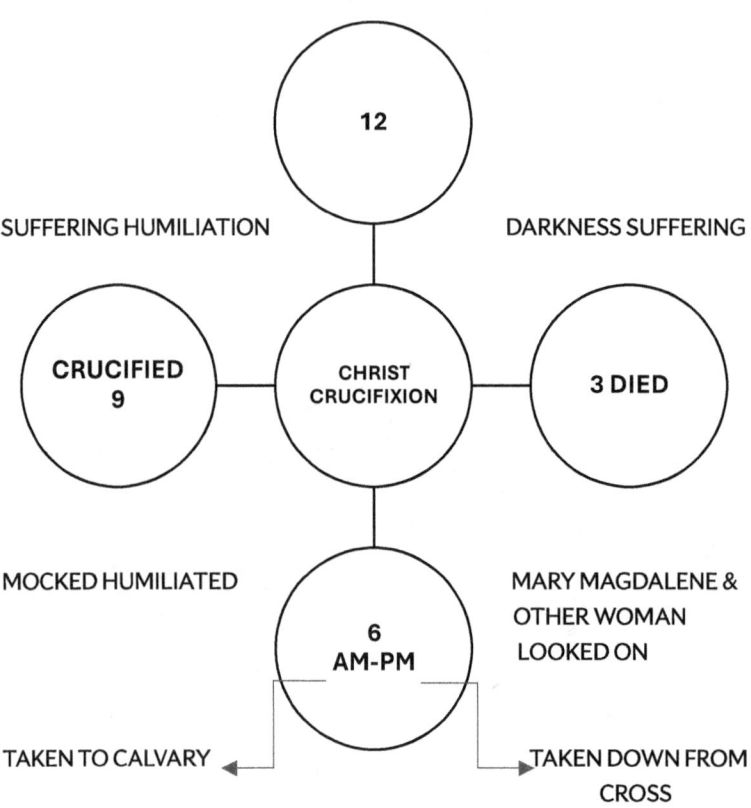

DARKNESS OVER THE LAND

6:00 am: Innocent Jesus was taken by misguided men to be crucified at Calvary (MK 15:1-20)

9:00 am: They crucified Jesus between two thieves, as a transgressor (Mark 15:25-27)

12:00 pm: Darkness covered the land from 12 noon (6th to 9th hr.) to 3:00 pm (MK 15:33)

3:00 pm: Jesus gave up the ghost (died on the cross) (Mark
           15:33-37)
           (The veil of the temple was rent in twain from top
           to bottom) (Mark 15:38)
           (A centurion exclaimed, "Truly, this man was the
           Son of God) (Mark 15:39)
           (There were women, including Mary Magdalene
           looking on afar off) (Mark 15:40)
6:00 pm: When the even was come Jesus' body was taken
           down by Joseph of Arimathea, an honorable
           counselor, who prepared his entombment at the
           sepulcher.

THE WHEEL OF LOVE
CAN YOU SEE THE CROSS?

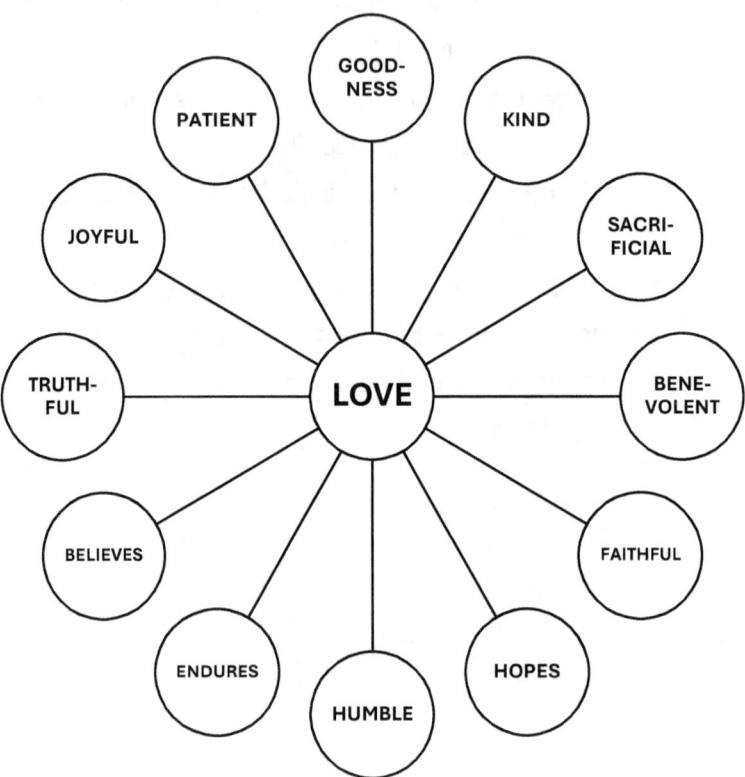

Love is the greatest value. It is descriptive of God: "He that loveth not knoweth not God; for God is love." (I" John 4:8). 1st John, Chapter 4, provides precious knowledge about love. This Wheel of Love is taken primarily from 1" Corinthians, Chapter 13. Many parents who love their children teach them to commit to memory, 1« Corinthians, Chapter thirteen. Without a doubt, 1" Corinthians, Chapter 13, ranks among the top universal classical literature expressions on the discourse of love. The ingredients and the characteristic of love enriches, nurtures and sustains our bodies, minds, souls, spirits and lives. The Creator expresses his love 10 to humanity through his excellency throughout the earth (Psalm 8:1), his heavens, the work of his fingers (Psalm 8:3-6), the moon and the stars that he has ordained. The same God who created the heavens and the earth, has sent a LOVE LETTER IN THE BIBLE AND HIS ONLY BEGOTTEN SON IN JESUS CHRIST TO ALL MANKIND. (John 3:16)

THE WHEEL OF SALVATION
CAN YOU SEE THE CROSS?

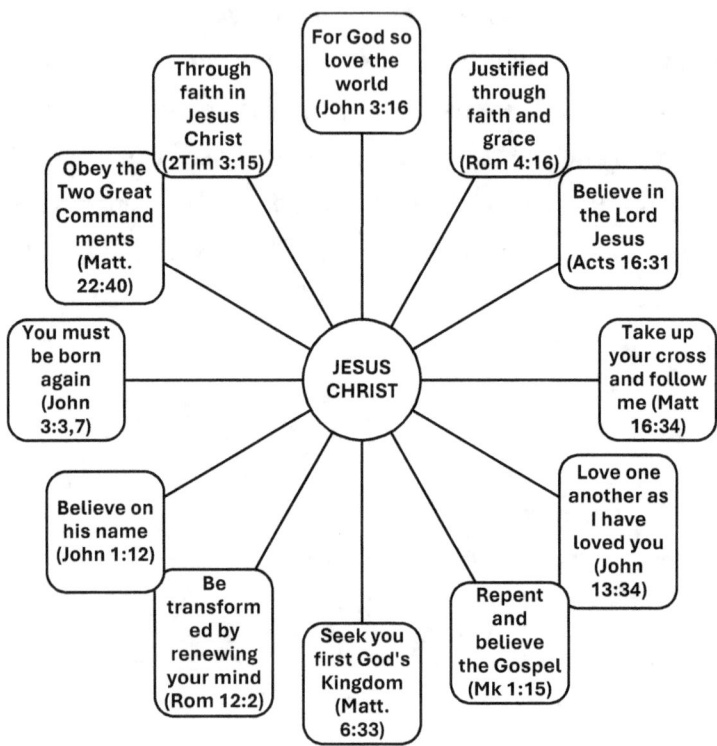

Every man, woman and child born into the world on this horizontal plane of earth needs salvation provided only by God. Every person is imprisoned by time, finiteness, mortality and the particularities of the circumstances of life. No person born into the world had any choice about their parents, race, place or circumstances of birth. At some point when the child discovers himself or herself they come to the realization that human beings such as themselves, have limited time and are forced to face the prospect of death. As the child grows and learns he or she realizes that there is no escape from death. No mortal knows what is on the other side. The child also learns that the journey of, "the shadow of death" must be taken alone. It is an individual, personal and private journey through the unknown. It happens to all people, regardless of their race, class, location or status in life. Medical doctors die. Presidents, preachers and prophets die. The child realizes that man on this horizontal level does not have the resources to overcome the prospect of death. The conscientious child begins to search for the answer to the serious and vital problem of mortality.

The child realizes that this problem of mortality is above the power of man. As the person ages, the search for the answer becomes more urgent. This life is such a precious gift that the desire for its continuation is a priority. Paul says, "But we have this treasure in earthen vessels, that the excellency of the power may be of God, and not of us." (2 Cor. 4-7). The GOOD NEWS OF THE BIBLE is that God has provided an answer. God knows that the body deteriorates over time and eventually, deceases. Sometimes death results from a multitude of other misfortunes. However, the loving God has provided a way to overcome the power of death. God provides a way of escape through the cross of Jesus Christ. There is a wheel of salvation in the cross of Christ. "For God so loved the world, that he gave his only begotten Son that whosoever believe in him should not perish, but have eternal life. (John 3:16).

The vertical dimension of the Cross symbolizes the salvation that God offers. It symbolizes God's lifeline (plumb line) handed down from above to rescue men, women, boys and girls from the doom of the secular horizontal world. God has made this salvation plan crystal clear through his creation, revelation and Jesus Christ. God has provided a way, "For this corruptible must put on incorruption, and this mortal must put on immortality (1 Corinthians 15:53). The Bible teaches that flesh and blood (1 Corinthians 15:50) cannot inherit the kingdom of God. The Bible teaches that there is a natural body (1 Cor. 15:44) and a spiritual body. God's salvation is for the whole person and the whole world. Salvation is available. The lifeline has been extended. The unmistakable message of God's Will for mankind has been given in the Holy Bible. Jesus is the Savior, the Way, Truth, Light and Life of the world. After two thousand years, no one else has come forth to make these claims. SALVATION IS AVAILABLE.

THE TIMELINE OF HISTORY
CAN YOU SEE THE CROSS?

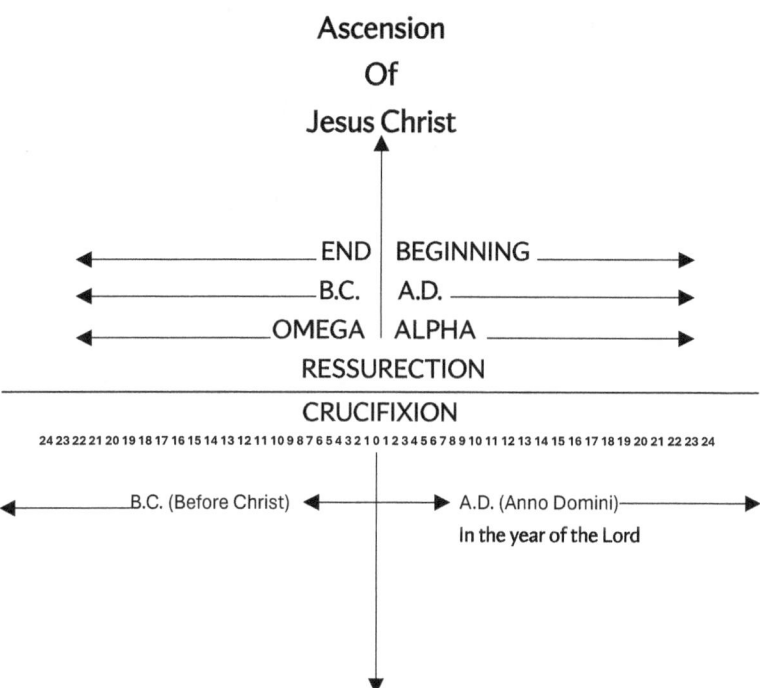

The advent of the birth of Jesus Christ created an indelible timeline of history on the earth. The calendars and the recorders of history began to count backward from Jesus' birth. They began to count forward from his birth. The backward count is known as B.C. (Before Christ). The forward count is known as A.D. (Anno Domini, Latin word for, in the year of our Lord. Jesus, literally, becomes the visible Alpha and Omega, the beginning and the end. The Word that became flesh and dwelt among us, ended the old and started the new, Jesus brought in the new age, the new dispensation, the new birth, new creatures, a new spiritual nature, a new heaven and a new earth. He is at the end of the old age and at the beginning of the new age. He came from eternity, was born in history, lived in taught for 33 years, was crucified in history, and resurrected in history on the horizontal plane. He taught and fellowshipped with his disciples for 40 days and ascended, "and a cloud received him out of their sight." (Actsl:9-11).

CONSTRUCT OF TRUE RELIGION
CAN YOU SEE THE CROSS?

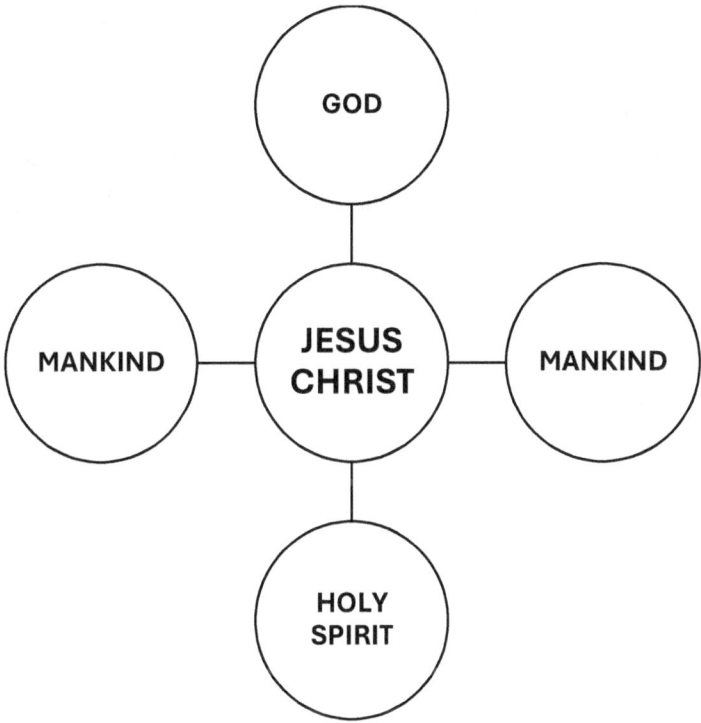

A religion that does not include God is not a valid religion. A religion that does not include men and women (humankind) is not a valid religion. A valid religion must have God. It must include men, women, boys and girls. The core meaning of religion is about mankind's relationship with God. This relationship consists of a vertical upreach to God from man. It consists of a horizontal outreach from humankind to humankind. It is a human outreach from human beings, one to another. It is a human outreach from human beings, one to another. It is a human upreach from mankind to God. It involves the vertical and horizontal connection of the cross. True religion involves man's relationship to the Triune God. This is confirmed by the words of Jesus: "Thou shall love the Lord thy God with all thy heart, and with all thy soul, and with all thy mind. This is the first and greatest commandment. And the second is like unto it, Thou shall love thy neighbor as thyself. On these two commandments hang all the law and the prophets." (Matthew 22:37-40).

THE WHEEL OF ART
CAN YOU SEE THE CROSS?

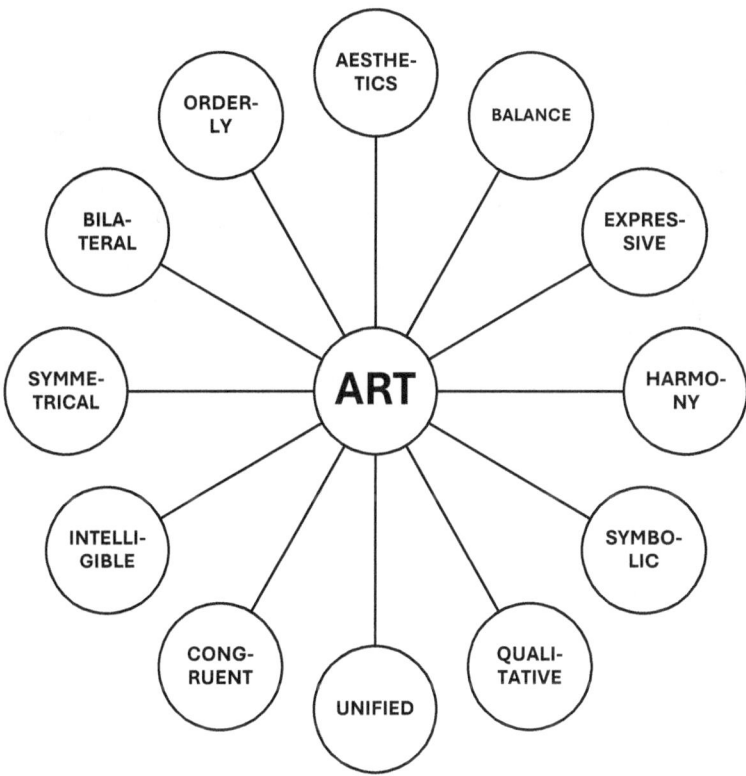

Art is self-evident in God's creation. It is observed in blue skies, the formation of clouds, sunsets and sunrises. It is seen in snowflakes, the sound of raindrops, and in the fall when the trees and vegetation change their colors. Art is expressed in the springtime when budding plants and blooming flowers come alive in their brilliant splendor. God's Word is an inexhaustible source of art. The Biblical Books of Job, Psalms, Proverbs, Ecclesiastes and Song of Solomon, are expressly rich with God-inspired art and wisdom. It is a tragedy that too many of our children are never exposed to the awe-inspiring and transforming art in Scripture. The Word of God through art has transforming power. It can be sung, taught, preached, chanted, written, painted, set to music, sculptured, dramatized, ornamentally designed, healed and inspired (God's Spiritual Prescriptions, W.J. Webb). The cross is a perfect form of art. God is an artist. "The Heavens declare the glory of God; and the firmament shows his handywork." (Psalms 19:1).

THE WHEEL OF SCIENCE
CAN YOU SEE THE CROSS?

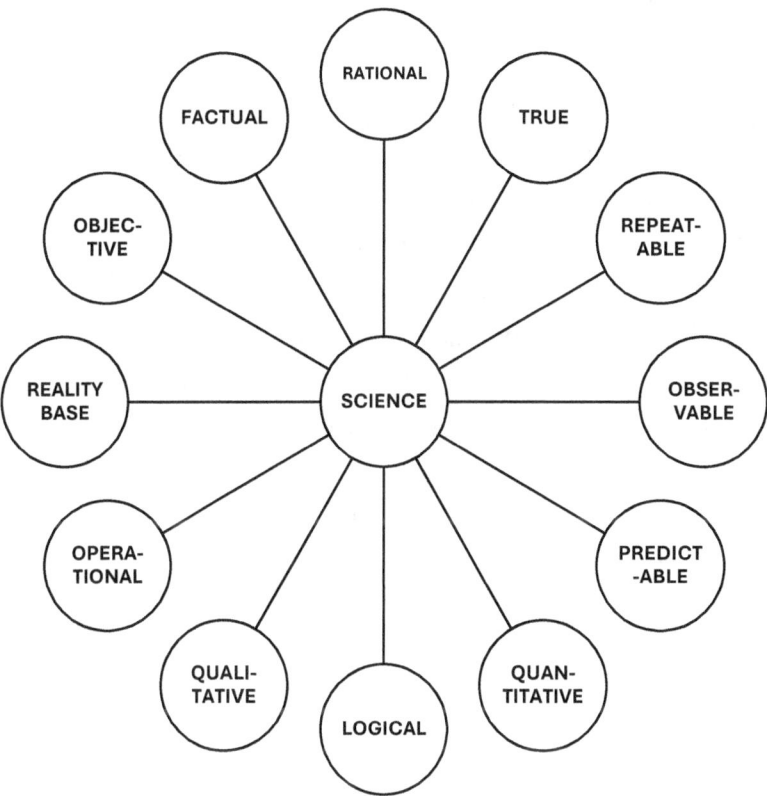

Science comes from the Latin word, Scientia, which means knowledge. Science has the capability of defining the nature of a specific entity based on available knowledge. Science uses observable and verifiable existing facts to specify and verify principles and truths through systematic methods of observation and study. True science and true religion are not in conflict with each other. It is pseudo-science and pseudo-religion that conflict. Man develops and uses science because God has established consistent gravitational, magnetic and other natural forces along with natural laws of physics, chemistry, biology and other sciences. God created man within an environment with a natural laboratory of infinite resources and possibilities. God blessed the man and the woman and commanded them to, "Be fruitful, and multiply, and replenish the earth, and subdue it: and have dominion over the fish of the sea, and over the fowl of the air, and over every living thing that moves upon the earth." (Gen. 1:28). God has provided man with religion, art, law and science to fulfill his commandment upon the earth. Science is an outpost of religion and therefore, must be theologically guided. Just as religion must answer to God, science, art and law must also answer to God. They are vehicular wheels created by God to bring salvation to mankind. Every wheel has a Cross.

WHEEL OF CHURCH LEADERSHIP
CAN YOU SEE THE CROSS?

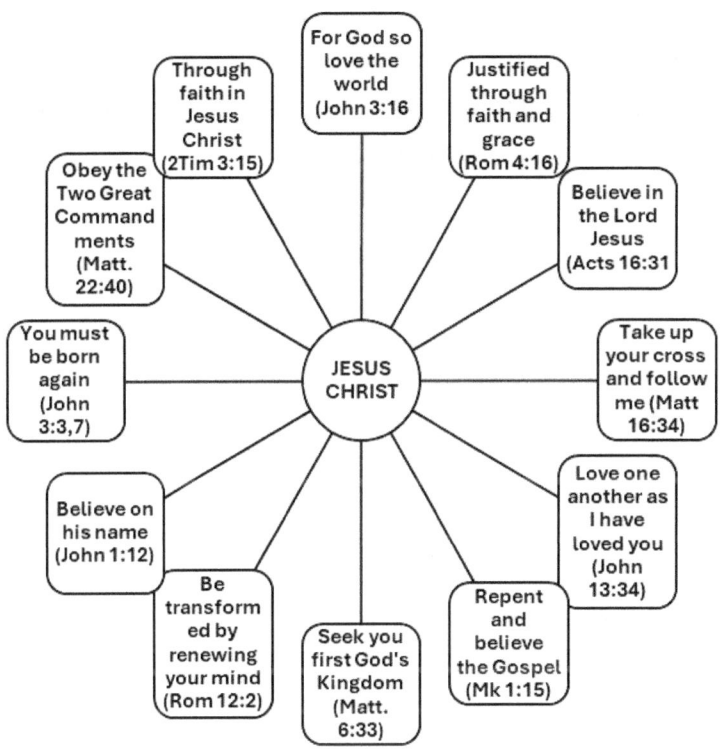

The mandate of the Church in this complex and perplexing 21st Century is to provide vital ideological, biblically-based leadership in all areas that impact on human life. Psalm 24 proclaims that the earth is the Lord's and the fullness thereof. Roman 13:1 mandates that, "every soul be subject unto the higher powers. For there is no power but of God: The powers that be are ordained by God." Jesus, who taught as one having authority (Matthew 7:29), stated after his resurrection

(Matthew 28:18-20), "All power is given unto me in heaven and in earth. Go ye therefore, and teach all nations, baptizing them in the name of the Father, and of the Son, and of the Holy Ghost... teaching them to observe all things, whatsoever I have commanded you." The Commands of Jesus are expressed in science, art, law and religion. There are no off-limits to the jurisdiction of God.

THE WHEEL OF PROFESSIONALISM
CAN YOU SEE THE CROSS?

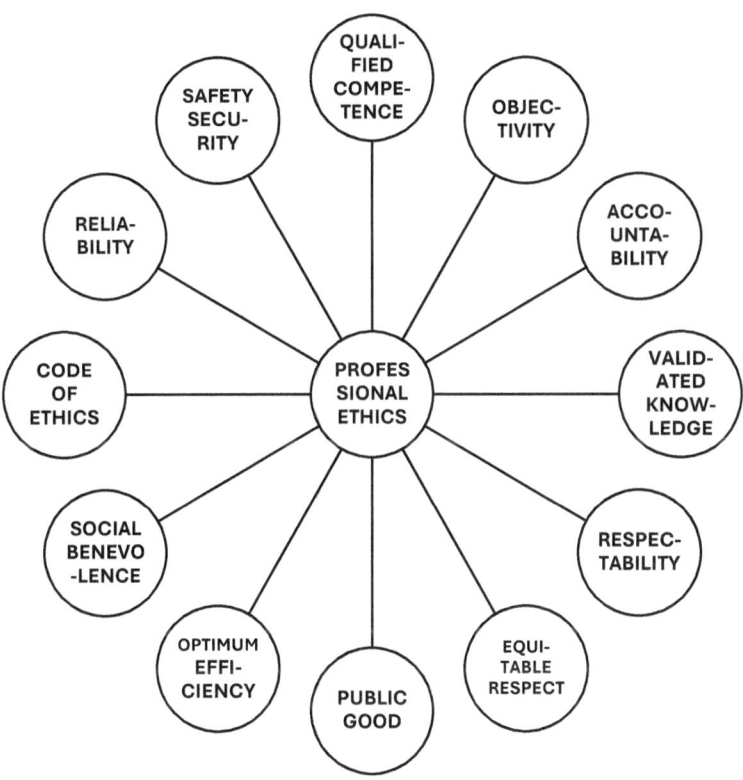

Professionalism promotes good business and good health. A professional and ethically operated business is efficient, productive, healthy and self-promoting. When people receive good services in a professional and efficient manner, they are likely to spread the good news to others. When individuals receive optimum benefits and minimum cost in their business and service transactions, they feel good. A good feeling in such an encounter is a health benefit. This health benefit can be multiplied. The promotion of professional and ethical practices in organizational and business enterprises can add significantly to the health of the Nation. (Excerpt from the book, The Way Out of Darkness, Willie James Webb). There is a great need to teach and practice this Wheel of Professionalism.

THE VOICE OF THE GREAT I AM
CAN YOU SEE THE CROSS?

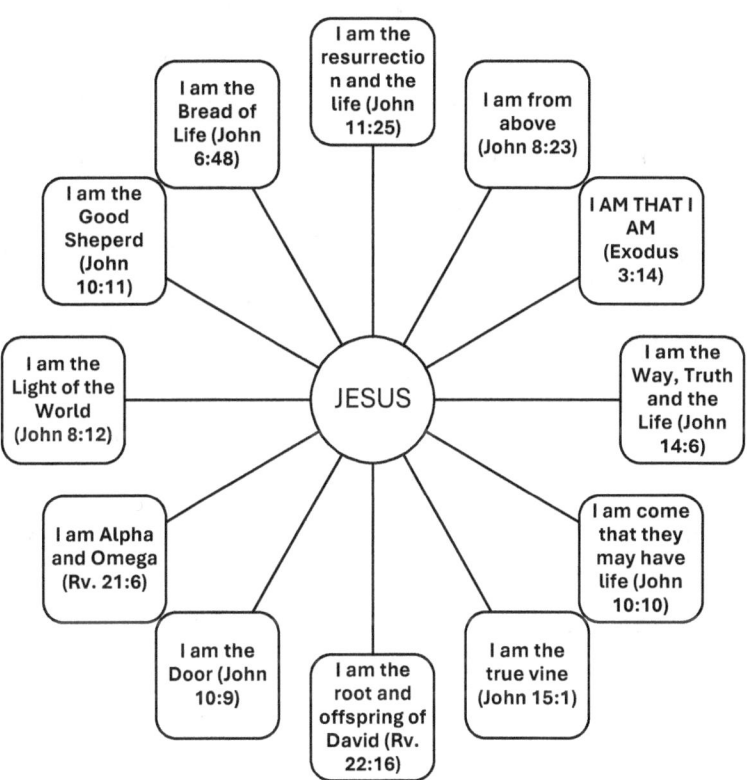

Jesus Christ is the only person in history that can make the claim of being the Great I Am with credibility. His claims are supported by the Bible, itself. "Neither is their salvation in any other; For there is none other names under heaven given among men, whereby we must be saved." (Acts 4:12). Gospels Matthew (Matthew 3:17), (Matthew 17:5), Mark

(Mark 1:11), (Mark 9:7), and Luke (Luke 3:22) record the voice of God from heaven stating, "This is my beloved son, in whom I am well pleased ... Hear him," in reference to Jesus Christ.

Matthew, Mark, Luke, John and Acts record numerous post-resurrection specific activities, places, teachings, instructions and commissions of Jesus Christ over 40 days after his resurrection. The evidence is invincible. The proof is infallible that Jesus rose from the dead and met with his disciples and others. Forty days after Jesus' resurrection he spoke promises to his disciples (Acts 1:8). And when he had spoken these things, while they beheld, he was taken up; and a cloud received him out of their sight. (Acts1:9).

The authenticity and truth of Jesus Christ are vindicated by all credible authoritative sources. He is vindicated by God, Law, Art, Science, religion, ethics and history. He is vindicated by the crucifixion, the resurrection, the cross and the ascension. Jesus Christ is the high priest. He is Lord of Lords and King of Kings. He is Mighty God, The Everlasting Father, The Prince of Peace. (Isaiah 9:6). Jesus Christ is the Great I AM.

Jesus Christ has put all enemies (1 Cor. 15:25) under his feet. He has put all things under his feet (1 Cor: 15:27; Ephesians 1:22). Jesus Christ is the GREAT I AM.

CHAPTER 6

THE INESCAPABLE CROSS

The cross is inescapable in the society, on earth and in the world. The cross is inextricably structured in God's creation. It is at the center and core of the physical world, the social world and spiritual world. It is at the core of mathematics, science, law, art and religion. It, the cross, is so interwoven and intertwined in the world, the envisionment and life itself, that it is an ever-present inexhaustible reality.

In order to understand the significance of the cross, we must view it in a broad sense. The cross came with creation. It is an intrical or inherent part of creation. It is a part of the celestial bodies. It is a part of every circle and spherical shape. It is involved in transactions, intersections and connections.

There is a cross at every intersection. Our cities are filled with crosses at every intersection. Even in the rural areas, there are cross roads, streets and expressways. There are railroad crossings. There are railroad tracks with cross ties. Cross ties are used under the two metal tracks that support the weight of trains. Ladders are constructed with vertical and horizontal connected supports of materials usually made of wood or metals. Airplanes are constructed as crosses. Airplanes are flying crosses. Airplanes are designed like birds.

When birds fly, they stretch their feet horizontally with their bodies and spread their wings and become a flying cross. When the bird lands, their legs become vertical. The landing plane lets down its wheels into a vertical position. Human beings are the only creatures on earth that are built to stand vertically erect. In the vertical erect position, a person becomes a cross when they stretch their arms straight out opposite each other.

The cross came when God created north, south, east and west. North, south, east and west are universal directions created by God and discovered by man. These four directions form the cross and their circular dimension forms the 360-degree circumference of the circle. Rounded global dimensions become spherical. Most of the celestial bodies are spherical shaped. The moon, planets and the sun are round spherical bodies. It is necessary to make this observation to understand another realization and revelation of the cross.

The phenomenon of the cross actively manifests itself on the Earth (as well as the planets and the moon) and in the sun. On the earth, the cross is manifested by gravity. Gravity is the force that holds everything, including rivers and oceans of water on a rounded spherical-shaped earth suspended in space (Job 26:7). The prophet Amos used a vision regarding the plumb line. Amos stated, "Thus he showed me: and behold, the Lord stood upon a wall made by a plumb line, with a plumb line in his hand." (Amos 7:7- 9). A plumb line (a free-floating suspended string) forms a straight line to earth by the force of gravity. Gravity pulls the string straight to the earth in a perpendicular fashion. This gravitational pull is proportionate around the Earth. Therefore, the opposite pulls or forces around the earth form crosses. This vision of the plumb line was observed by the prophet Amos in the 8 century B.C. The same gravitational force causes the leveling instrument to achieve accurate measures in construction. The leveling instrument is (usually) a straight-edged material with a glass tube or transparent plastic that contains a bubble that designates when a surface is level. The gravitational force has opposite correlates around the Earth.

The huge glowing ball, the sun at the center of our solar system, sends out light, heat and other forms of energy in all directions. Light travels in straight lines. Therefore, it is logical and reasonable to conclude that the trillions or zillions of light rays have opposites or correlates in all directions around the sun. Therefore, crosses exist all around the sun. The sun is round and spherical, and therefore it has a center with a radius, diameter, and circumference like other celestial bodies. The volume of the sun is over a million times larger than the Earth. (World Book Encyclopedia). Considering God's marvelous and astounding creation, it is no wonder that the Psalmist exclaimed, "When I consider thy heavens, the work of thy fingers, the moon and the stars, which thou hast ordained; what is a man that thou art mindful of him?" (Psalm 8:3-4).

There are many interesting and significant volumes of writing on various subjects regarding the cross. However, this book proposes to show that the cross existed before Christianity or even humanity itself. The Romans were crucifying persons convicted under their law long before Jesus was born. The Romans did not limit their crucifixions to just persons identified as Christians on the cross. The use of the cross to crucify persons found guilty of certain capital offenses had a long history by the Romans long before the Christians came on the historical scene.

There is evidence to suggest that many persons are offended by the cross in the context of it being a Christian symbol. The cross is acknowledged as a Christian symbol but not restricted to a Christian symbol. Strangely, the anti-cross is synonymous with anti-Christ. Strangely, anti-cross and anti-Christ are more pronounced than anti-crucifixion or anti-persecution.

There is a need to explore the reasons and rationale of those who are anti-cross and anti-Christ. Why the animosity against the cross of Christ? Why the hatred towards Jesus, who, as an innocent Son of God, was crucified on the cross? Where is the animosity towards the laws, the government, the citizens and the religion that either participated or watched silently and indifferently while innocent Jesus was being crucified? Why this misdirected hatred towards the righteousness, goodness and will of God? Are not their other things that are harmful to life, threats to safety and security that are more in need of hating and restricting than the Cross of Christ? Children are being neglected. The lines of the hungry, helpless and hopeless are getting longer. The school dropout rate is increasing. The school achievement rate is declining. There are health epidemics, drug abuse and crime throughout the nation. Terroristic threats, wars and rumors of wars are raging. Why this hatred for the cross of Christ and the Prince of Peace in Christ? The above questions call for a close and thorough examination of our individual selves, the church, the society, the government and the nation, itself. What are our motives in spending as much time, energy and resources to get away from the inescapable cross?

CHAPTER 7

THE BIBLE'S SPIRITUAL AUTHORSHIP

The spiritual authorship of the Bible extends beyond sixteen hundred years. Humanity knows of no other written document with the continuity, congruence and progressive revelation as is contained in the sixty-six books of the Bible.

There is a spirit behind the authorship of books. There is a master spirit behind the content of literary works. The book or the literary work, itself, will reveal something about the author. Books reveal many things about their authors. Books reveal literary style, themes, perspectives, flavor, intentions and rationale. Books often reveal the character, morality, will, intent, purpose and spiritual identification of the author.

It makes for very interesting studies and discussions to analyze and discuss various books and other literary works. That is not the intent of this chapter. Most people will agree that the books and other literary works and even other artistic works that you produce will reveal something about you and your identification. This brief scenario is provided to establish a foundation to discuss the Spiritual Authorship of the Bible. I approach this subject with great humility. I acknowledge that there are more scholarly persons, theologically, who could do a much better job than myself. My primary objective is to raise the consciousness of the Nation regarding the Spiritual Authorship of the Bible.

There is strong infallible evidence that the Holy Spirit of God is the Author of the Bible. Peter says, "For the prophecy came not in old time by the will of man: but holy men of God spoke as they were moved by the Holy Ghost." (2 Peter 1:21). Paul says in second Timothy, "All scripture is given by inspiration of God, and is profitable for doctrine, for reproof, for correction, for instruction in righteousness." (2 Timothy 3:16).

The Bible has come to be regarded by too many persons as being just one of the holy books along with the holy books of other religions. The American democratic form of government along with a questionable doctrine of "separation of Church and State." reinforces the relegation of the Bible as just another holy book along with many others. Objective religious theological scholars in world religion have come to the conclusion that the Judeo-Christian Bible is unique and there is no other book or holy writ that compares to the Bible. The Bible reveals the monotheistic, omnipotent creator and sovereign God of the universe and of the earth. The Judeo-Christian Bible reveals a God who participates in the affairs of man on the earth. This God sends prophets, messengers and angels to communicate instructions, commandments and prophecies to mankind.

The Eternal God

According to (Genesis 1:1) God has no beginning. (Genesis 1:1) says, "In the beginning God created the heaven and the earth." This Scripture suggests a beginningless eternity before God created the heaven and the earth. God created the beginning. Clearly, God is the omnipotent, omniscient, omnipresent, infinite, immortal, creator and eternal God. God's sovereignty, authority, power and jurisdiction are from everlasting to everlasting.

This description and revelation of God in the Bible is congruent with and conforms to the "handywork" of God in the universe (Psalm 19:1). Man is able to see the miraculous, amazing creation of God in the stars and the vastness of space. God reveals his wonders on the earth. The planet Earth, the moon, the other planets and the brilliance of the sun dazzles and stagger the most exaggerated imagination.

We cannot begin to describe all the wonders of the earth. It has mountains, valleys, forests, rivers, lakes, streams and oceans of water all around the spherical-shaped earth. From the bosom of the earth there are gems of gold, silver, diamonds and other precious stones. There are beautiful plants, multivariety of flowers, roses, fruits and vegetables. The earth is habituated with extensive animal life on the land, in the waters and in the air.

What is Man?

It is no wonder that the Psalmist raises the question, "What is man, that thou are mindful of him? And the son of man, that thou visitist him?" (Psalm 8:4)

The Psalmist seems to detect that God has a special affinity or favor towards man. The Psalmist seems to realize that God has placed man in a special place within the scheme of God's Creation.

The Psalmist continues and says, "For thou has made him a little lower than the angels and hast crowned him with glory and honor." (Psalm 8:5).

"Thou madest him to have dominion over the works of thy hands; thou hast put all things under his feet." (Psalm 8:6)

It is interesting to notice that the Psalmist is communicating with God. The Psalmist is addressing God. There is a spiritual connection between the spirit of the Psalmist and the Spirit of God.

Spirit of Love and Concern

The Master Holy Spirit of the Bible expresses a persisting, agonizing love and concern for man. The Bible expresses God's concern for the total welfare and wellbeing of man. God created man (Genesis 1:27) in his own image and gave him blessings and dominion (Genesis 1:28) over all creatures of the earth.

God made Adam a helpmeet in the woman Eve (Genesis 2:21-24) and placed them in a garden of paradise (Genesis 2:15). They disobeyed God and were driven out of the garden (Genesis 3:24).

This loving and agonizingly concerned God has given man rich and true instructions and righteous and just values for living. He has provided man with bountiful resources for living. He sent prophets to warn man of the consequences of his disobedience and rebellion. God sent his only Begotten Son to save man and give him eternal life.

The same loving and redemptive Spirit that authored the Bible and sent the Savior, Jesus Christ, two thousand years ago is that same loving and redemptive Spirit that is speaking to man in this 21st century.

The Bible is an on-target documentation of God's love and concern for man, and man's continuous rejection of God's love and willful disobedience to God. It is so interesting that the same picture of the disobedience of Adam and Eve and the succeeding generations is the same picture portrayed in America and the world today in the 21st century.

The creator of the universe is still speaking through the heavens, the stars, the moon, the solar system and the earth. God is still speaking through earthquakes, floods, tornadoes and other natural disasters, signs and wonders in an effort to get man's attention.

Unfortunately, man does not hear God's voice or connect with the message of God in the outer world of nature. God's prophets, his message and Jesus Christ are still speaking through the Bible.

The Wakeup Call

God used a whirlwind out of the north, a great cloud, an unfolding fire and a brightness and the likeness of four living creatures with wheels (Ezekiel 1:4-20) that got the attention of Ezekiel. After Ezekiel observed the revelation of this spectacular happening, God told Ezekiel to stand upon his feet and God would speak to him. The spirit entered into Ezekiel as God spoke to him. God told Ezekiel that he would send Ezekiel to the children of Israel, a rebellious nation that had transgressed against God as their fathers did (Ezekiel 2:1-7). God described the children of Israel as impudent children and stiff hearted (Ezekiel 2:4).

It was important to God to send Ezekiel to Israel to let them know that God has a prophet among them. He sent Ezekiel to warn the children of Israel. God wanted Israel to be warned whether they listened to the warning or not listen. God wanted Israel to know that death is the consequence of wickedness.

The Duty to Warn

God made Ezekiel a watchman unto the house of Israel and gave Ezekiel the duty to warn Israel (Ezekiel 3:17-21) of their wickedness. If Ezekiel failed to warn Israel as directed by God then the wicked who die without warning, God will require accountability on the part of Ezekiel. God requires that the wicked be warned of the consequences of death due to their iniquity. God also wants the wicked to know that if they turn from their wickedness they can live.

The message of Ezekiel is that God loves Israel and God wants Israel to be fully warned of the lethal dangers of sin and iniquity. God wants Israel to be saved. Ezekiel makes the salvation message clear for Israel. However, this message is relevant today for all people.

Salvation in Christ

Jesus was born about 600 years after the prophecy of Ezekiel (597 B.C.). Ezekiel's prophecy to warn the wicked to turn from their wickedness and iniquity is still relevant. However, the coming of Christ has increased the duty to spread the word of God and to expand it to all people and all nations. In the day of Ezekiel, God wanted Israel to know that a prophet was among them. After the coming of Jesus Christ, God wants the world to know that there is a Savior; God's only Begotten Son, Jesus Christ, is among God's people and he reigns forever with God. Jesus Christ is the Good News For All People! God created the universe. God authored the Bible. God's Word became flesh in Christ (John 1:14).

Duty to Witness

Go ye therefore, and teach all nations, baptizing them in the name of the Father, and of the Son, and of the Holy Ghost: Teaching them to observe all things whatsoever I have commanded you: and, lo, I am with you always, even unto the end of the world (Matthew 28:19-20).

CHAPTER 8

REVELATIONS OF THE CROSS

There are too many revelations of the cross to include in a single volume. This chapter will be a general summarized overview of some of the revelations of the cross. First, we make the distinction between the general revelations of the cross and the cross of Christ. As we have illustrated in previous chapters, the cross is a universal configuration that predates the birth of Christ and also predates the creation of man and religion. The cross is a part of creation and the natural order.

Summary of Natural Revelations

A wheel is round and circular. The intersection of the vertical line and the horizontal line creates four 90-degree angles which make a cross. These four right angles of 90 degrees make a complete circle. A straight line of 180 degrees and the 360-degree circle is universal. That fact came with creation. The wheel is an invention of man. However, the "wheel in the middle of a wheel," was used by God to get Ezekiel's attention. God created roundness with creation. Roundness is the primary shape of celestial bodies. The earth, moon, other planetary bodies and the sun are round-shaped. Round and spherical-shaped objects have centers, diameters, radiuses and circumferences. Right angles and other intersecting angles can be computed to form crosses. The four universal directions of north and south (vertical) and east and west (horizontal) form a cross.

The cross represents balance and symmetry. The circle represents wholeness and completion. The balance and symmetry make the wheel run, roll, turn, spin or revolve smoothly. God's creation is dynamic. Everything is suspended in space. Nothing is tied down. Everything is moving and changing. The balance of the cross and the turning and revolving of the wheel are used to measure, quantify and identify.

God's celestial bodies are moving, changing and rotating. The movement and the rotation of the earth give us four seasons every 365 days of rotation around the sun. The clock is designed for 12 hours of daylight and 12 hours of night. The addition of the two equals one twenty-four-hour day. The complete revolution of 60 minutes equals one hour on the clock.

Hopefully, sufficient information has been shared to see clearly that there is a divine history and purpose behind the cross and the wheel. They are not arbitrary configurations. They have significant messages for mankind. They can be used to measure, quantify and identify. When we can use a vertical line and change a negative minus sign to a positive plus sign we know that there is science in the cross. When we can see balance, harmony and congruence in the circle, we know that there is art in the cross. When we see the wheels of justice turning and when they stop evenly and balanced, we know that justice and judgment can be found in the cross. When we can see in the cross, the horizontal outreach to man and the vertical downreach from God, we know that there is love in the cross.

If you are lost and need to find your way, there is a compass on the cross. It points north, south, east, west and all points in between.

If you want to know what time it is, look at the cross. There is a time piece and clock in the cross.

If you want to learn about God's Lifeline through God's Plumb Line, look at the cross. There is a life line in the cross.

If you want to learn about justice, injustice and the scales of justice take a closeup look at the cross.

If you want to study the time line of history, B.C. and A.D., Alpha and Omega, the beginning and the end, study the cross.

If you want to learn about the depths of love, the love of man and the love of God, look at the weight and the sacrifice of the cross.

If you want to learn about God's salvation, the way, the truth and the life. look at the cross. There is a salvation plan in the cross.

If you want to see the meeting place of the secular and the sacred, the material and the spiritual, hatred and love, man and God, time and eternity, light and darkness, life and death, look at the cross.

The cross is certainly a universal symbol and reality. It can be observed, demonstrated and illustrated through science, art, law and religion. The significance and power of the cross cannot be fully understood and expressed by man. Paul understood that we do not know everything about the cross. He was also aware that the cross of Christ may seem foolish to the world. "But unto us which are saved it is the power of God." (1 Corinthians 1:18).

Why the Offense of the Cross?

It has been made obvious in the public square that there is animosity against the cross. There have been lawsuits to remove crosses from the grave sites of deceased veterans in National Cemeteries and from mountains where crosses were placed as memorials to the American war dead. As reasonable people reflect on the expressed hostilities and animosities toward the public display of the cross, something appears to be out of proportion logically as well as ideologically. What is there about a cross that could offend someone. Crosses are pervasive throughout our cities at every intersection and four way stop signs. We have benevolent agencies known as The Red Cross, The White Cross, Blue Cross, Blue Shield. Plus signs and time signs are common mathematical symbols. Most airplanes have the aerodynamic shape of a flying cross. Crosses are found in window panes and doors. Every circle has 4 right angles that form a cross.

No, it is not the configuration of the cross that they hate. They hate their contrivance of the religious symbol of the cross. Specifically, they hate the cross of Christ. Paul gives us some insight into the hatred of the cross of Christ, (For many walk, of whom I have told you often, and now tell you even weeping, that they are the enemies of the Cross of Christ.). (Philippians 3:18). There is something about the Cross of Christ that is hated.

Jesus gives additional light on the subject in the Gospel of John when he says, "If I had not come and spoken unto them, they had not had sin: but now they have no cloke for their sin." (John 15:22).

These words of Jesus suggests strongly that men want a covering for their sin and wrong doing. Somehow, the Cross of Christ is a reminder that the crime of the persecution and the crucifixion of Christ was not successfully covered up. Their plans to cover up their crimes with the crucifixion, the ultimate capital punishment did not work. Those who hate truth and disbelieve God are disappointed and baffled that the crucifixion of Jesus on the cross did not end the life of Jesus. They don't want to be reminded that the cross failed them. The cross failed to stop Jesus. It failed to stop the truth and the good news of God for the righteous. The cross failed to put out the light. The cross brought lighter on their evil deeds. This spectacular crucifixion on Calvary in public during the day light hours failed. The believers in Christ embraced his sacrifice on the cross for the sins of the world. For the unbelievers, the cross disappointed and let them down. They became enemies to the Cross of Christ. The resurrection of Jesus shattered their dark world of wickedness and evil. In their rebellion against God and their denial of the resurrection of Jesus Christ, they became enemies to the cross.

The Grand Conspiracy

The street criminals, or people from the lower socio-economic groups or lower class did not crucify Christ. It was the top echelon of the Greco-Roman World that crucified Christ. The Holy Land was located in a rich cultural and enlightened world. It was influenced by the great civilizations of the Greeks, Egyptians, Africans and Romans. Socrates, Aristotle, Plato and other Greek thinkers lived several centuries before Christ. Imperial Rome had the most advanced statutory Laws and government. The Jews had the most enlightened religion.

This is the perplexing question: How could a knowledgeable and culturally enlightened society with the most advanced statutory laws and government, along with the most advanced religion, Judaism, collaborate, conspire and crucify a totally innocent man? This totally innocent man was Jesus Christ.

The accusation, persecution, conviction and crucifixion of innocent people sends a very sobering and disturbing message. The message is this, that the institutions of men cannot be trusted.

Your leaders, educational institutions, religious institutions and government bureaucracies cannot be trusted with your rights, your liberty and your life. If the educational, legislative, executive, judicial, religious, business and the silence of the crowd, let Jesus down, the Son of God, what about the common people?

The Pharisees and Sadducees represented religion. They brought accusations against Jesus to Pilate who represented the government. Pilate acknowledged there was no credible evidence against Jesus. He could have released Jesus. He was more interested in placating the religious leaders and the crowd than he was about the rights and the life of Jesus. Pilate suggested the release of Jesus according to one of their customs that allowed for the release of a criminal. The crowd was against the release of Jesus who was innocent. The crowd was in favor of the release of a real criminal, Barabbas. Pilate, in his weakness and irresponsibility, gave the choice to the crowd, whether they wanted Jesus or Barabbas released. Pilate negated his responsibility as a government leader and allowed a manipulated misguided mob to make the decision to release Barabbas. Pilate appealed to the crowd to make the second decision, "what shall I do then with Jesus, which is called Christ?" (Matthew 27:22). Their answer was, "Let him be crucified."

The intervention of God through the resurrection of Jesus Christ averted the greatest potential coverup in history. The resurrection of Jesus vindicated the truth of his ministry and the identity of his person as the only Begotten Son of God. This was an Act of God for humanity.

Hope in the Cross

The Cross of Christ was a place where darkness was transformed into eternal light. Suffering and sacrifice were transformed into eternal salvation. The dead-end street of death at the cross became an open door and highway to heaven. The Cross of Christ represents the worst human tragedy of injustice and man's inhumanity to man. Jesus makes all things new. He creates a new heaven and a new earth. He transforms, at the cross, a place of crucifixion and death into a place of resurrection and eternal life.

Core Message

God, the creator of reality and existence, is inescapable. God's special creation of man, a creature with unlimited potential, was made in the image of God. God has revealed and demonstrated his love, generosity, patience and mercy for man for over five thousand years of history. And yet, man through his denial, disobedience and rebellion against God, languishes in spiritual infantilism. This arrogant refusal and failure to grow up spiritually, mentally and emotionally, has put civilization and the earth at risk for destruction. THE FINAL CALL TO WAKE UP, GROW UP AND STAND UP IS NOW!

God gave man every potential to grow up and build a paradise and kingdom of God on earth. However, these spiritual infants are creating an anti-God, anti-Bible, anti-Christ, anti-cross and unholy, unsacred and unrighteous technological playpen on the earth. It just so happens that the playpen includes a nuclear arsenal and other weapons of mass destruction. The technological, socio-cultural and geo-political developments on the earth have progressed beyond the intellectual, emotional, moral and ethical capacity of man to manage and guide responsibly. The wheel of life on Earth is spinning out of control.

The growing impending Crises of America and the nations of the earth are so deep and perplexing that the only way out is a Biblically based God solution. THE ANSWERS ARE IN THE WORD OF GOD.

God is inescapable. "For in him we live, and move, and have our being." (Actsl7:28).

How shall we escape, if we neglect so great salvation? (Hebrews 2:3)

W. J. Webb

BIBLIOGRAPHY AND REFERENCES

American Psychiatric Association. (1994). Diagnostic and Statistical Manual of Mental Disorders (4th ed.). Washington, DC: Author.

Benne, Robert. The Paradoxical Vision, A Public Theology for the Twenty-first Century. Fortress Press. 1955.

The Holy Bible (King James Version)

Buttrick, George Arthur (ed.) The Interpreters Bible. New York: Abingdon Press, 1952.

Carter, Stephen L. The Culture of Disbelief. New York: Random House, 1994.

Curran, Linda A. Trauma Competency: A Clinician's Guide. Eau Claire, 2010.

Everly, George S., Jr. Personality-Guided Therapy for Posttraumatic Stress Disorder. Washington, DC: American Psychological Association. 2004.

Fosdick, Harry Emerson. The Modern Use of the Bible. New York: McMillan Co. 1961,

Strong, James. The New Strongs Exhaustive Concordance. Nashville: Nelson Publishers, 1995.

Thiemann, Ronald F. Constructing a Public Theology. Louisville: John Knox Press, 1991.

Twerski, Abraham J. Addictive Thinking: Understanding Self-Deception. Center City, Minnesota: Hazelden, (1990).

Webb, Willie J. God's Spiritual Prescriptions. Atlanta, Georgia

Webb. Willie J. Psychotrauma-The Human Injustice Crisis. Lima, Ohio: Fairway Press. 1990.

Webb, Willie James. The Way Out of Darkness. Atlanta, Georgia

The World Book Encyclopedia. (1992). Chicago, London, Toronto, Sydney: World Book Inc.

www.ingramcontent.com/pod-product-compliance
Lightning Source LLC
Chambersburg PA
CBHW060532130626
46553CB00002B/716